By Robert Pelton

ORIGINAL PUBLICATIONS

PLAINVIEW, NEW YORK

ISBN: 0-942272-50-1

TABLE OF CONTENTS

PREFACE

The word "amulet" comes from the Arabian *hamala* which simply means to carry something on the person. Amulets have always been extremely popular among Voodooists. They are charms or other objects which are usually hung on a string or chain around the neck, or tied to the wrist. Many amulets are secretly carried in the hair, in a pocket, or pinned to the clothing. Voodoo amulets are designed to ward off evil spirits which cause sickness, injury and death—and they are also worn as portents of good fortune. Many early Voodoo Kings and Queens were specialists in creating amulets of all sorts. These would include such names as Marie Comtesse, Eliza, Malvina Latour, Don Pedro, Doctor Yah Yah, Leon Janpier and Doctor Beuregard.

Some practioners of Voodoo are referred to as "living a charmed life,"which implies a seeming immunity from danger, accidents and illness. Mistakes are seldom made and decisions always seem to be the right ones. All of these individuals make it a habit to wear some sort of a charm to help ensure this end.

A great number of Voodoo charms are engraved with peculiar figures and symbols. This type charm is most commonly known as a talisman and are believed by the owner to possess special supernatural powers. Such talismans are said to prevent losses, help avoid injuries, overcome illnesses, etc. They keep evil away from the wearer and help effect disease cures. Others are designed to attract good luck, bring financial gain, create love spells, develop sensuality, etc. Voodoo talismans are often carefully engraved on a special seal, medallion, or semi-precious stone or are embroidered on cloth. They are most commonly worn on the finger as a ring, on a chain or string around the neck, or carried in a purse or pocket.

Astrological rings are commonly worn by members of Voodoo cults, as are other rings set with certain precious stones. One or more mystical symbols are often engraved on the stone or on the ring itself. The stone and the metal of the ring conforms to the sign of the particular planet or to the birth sign of the wearer. Such jewelry is believed to exert a powerful influence on the character and conduct of the person who possesses it. Thus it is said to bring the owner luck and protection against all harm. There are innumerable old Voodoo beliefs regarding the wonderful and disasterous effects of these special charms and talismans. The notorious Doctor John, bearded Voodoo High Priest in New

Orleans in the 1800's, dabbled in astrology as a part of his fantastic practice.

Precious, semi-precious gems and other stones in general have an important place in Voodoo tradition and belief. Certain ones are believed to have a special province in inducing fortunate or unfortunate occurrences. Lodestone was commonly prescribed by Sanite Dede, New Orleans' most frightful Voodoo Queen of the early 1800's. Proper stones are selected according to the month of one's birth, because of the supernatural power attributed to it, or because it happens to be a favorite of some specific *loa* (spirit). *Bluestone was* often used by Regina Nicaud who worked for High Priestess Mamma Antoine, before finally becoming a Voodoo Queen herself in the 1870's.

The practice of making and using charms, amulets and talismans is an ancient Voodoo art. It was carried over from Africa to the West Indies where it is still prevalent And today, as in early Louisiana history, it is of extreme popularity throughout the United States. Modern Voodooists,. as well as numerous other people, still wear or carry some sort of amulet or talisman, for the most part in secrecy. They may not actually believe completely in its efficacy as the true Voodoo practitioner does, but do desire to gain the benefit of the charm or amulet in case it should possess some hidden supernatural virtue.

Candles have always had a peculiar spiritualistic character. This is true with regard to Voodoo as well as all other religious and occult sects. Candles are now and have from time immemorial been used for sacred rituals and rites. Candles are often used as charms because of their attributed spiritual, vibratory influences. It is customary in Voodoo to bring candles to ceremonies in honor of one's favorite *loa* (spirit) ot patron saint. The size of the candle, its color, and how it is decorated are taken as signs of the owner's belief, enthusiasm and purpose or need. Many unusual superstitions are gleaned from the use of candles and such items have always been used as an important part of *every* ritual conducted by High Priests and Priestesses of American Voodoo.

The fear of what is commonly called the *evil eye is* very prevalent in Voodoo today. Certain individuals are believed to possess an evil eye with which they are able to hex or cast a curse on anyone at any time. It is usually accomplished by merely staring at the person with intense hatred or jealousy. Marie Laveau, one of the best known High Priestesses of the past, is said to have possessed a terrible evil eye. This famous Voodoo Queen was feared by all between the late 1820's and 1869 when she was made to involuntarily retire.

A great number of powerful charms, talismans and amulets have been designed to counteract the bad effects of such a horrible curse. Reverend Father Joe Watson, a Voodoo conjurer of the 1930's, claimed to be able to lift any hex no matter how powerful it was or who placed it. A jet (velvet-black mineral) cross is frequently used in Voodoo as a means to achieve this end. Such a cross is believed to work wonders in overcoming the dastardly effects of an evil eye curse. It is said to shatter Unsplit when looked upon by anyone with evil intent.

The Voodoo belief in horseshoes as an emblem of good luck can readily be traced to ancient African phallic worship. The peculiar shape of the horseshoe represents. sex and potency among Voodo6 practitioners. It is a very old object of superstitous belief and occult lore. Horseshoes, by and large, have always denoted an influence for good rather than evil. This type object is still extremely popular in Voodoo belief and practice today. Many rituals which include phallic worship are included in the subsequent chapters.

The cross, an emblem of Christianity, has served as the source of many superstitions and supernatural beliefs. Even in Voodoo it is considered to attract good fortune and ward off all evil. Contrary to the generally accepted belief, the cross did not have its origin as an emblem of Christianity. Africans, when missionaries first landed, possessed similar devices. Men of the cloth found the cross universally adopted by most African tribes. This led some of them to claim that the devil had given it to the uncivilized blacks in order to damn them with a false religion like Voodoo. The cross, however, was associated through much of history with phallic worship.

Charms made of wood are often worn around the neck on chains or a piece of string. The wearer will then have it handy when needed to draw good fortune or stop evil doings. Many blacks in the old South wore one wooden button sewn on their coat or some other piece of clothing. This was believed to bring success in everything undertaken, and to lose a wooden button signified complete failure and danger to come.

In the following pages I have tried to cover the practice of Voodoo as it was developed by the most notable practitioners in our history, such names as those mentioned previously and many others including Doctor Jack, Joseph Melon, Doctor Sol, Doc Alexander, Mamie Hughes,Marie Saloppe and Helen Thomas. The bock also attempts to show the reader how to actually make these various black and white magic items correctly. And it clearly explains how they are to be worn or otherwise used in an effort to gain certain supernatural powers. Included are concise biographical sketches cf the important Priests and Priestesses or Kings and Queens of American Voodoo, most of which you will no doubt be meeting for the first time. You wild find documented evidence of where, when and how the magic of Voodoo was implemented, by whom, and with what success.

This book is designed to be a guide for both the neophyte and the already experienced practitioner. The proper techniques are well illustrated, and the directions are easy to follow. Any reader can, through correct and diligent application of these instructions, successfully master this age-old magical art.

1

To Place a Curse

TO DRAW AND DIRECT EVIL FORCES

This talisman gives its possessor the power of directing all infernal forces of evil against his or her enemies. It is said to be one of the most powerful hexing methods in Voodoo. Embroider in ***black silk on gray satin*** and carry with you. It may also be engraved on a ring or an amulet.

Note: The two snakes represent Agarou Tonnerre, one of the most dangerous and powerful of all evil Voodoo loas (spirits). The duck on the water represents *Simi,* a water loa-with clairvoyant powers who aids in directing the evil forces of Agarou Tonnerre. The other symbols are simply made to encase the evil power of the talisman, in order to protect the wearer from its potential destructiveness. Agarou Tonnerre demands an offering of a black rooster while Simi requires a dish of burning charcoal before either of them will take any positive action on the wearer's behalf. The rooster must be put to death and his still warm blood tasted by everyone taking part in the ritualistic offering.

POWERFUL CURSING CHARM

This is a powerful Voodoo curse attributed to Marie Laveau, one of New Orleans most notorious Voodoo Queens in the 1800's. It should be used with great caution. Start by blending the following ingredients. They are to be mixed only at midnight.

Asafoetida	**A pinch**
Black Arts Oil	**3 drops**
Crossing Incense	**1 tablespoon**
JuJu Oil	**3 drops**
Hair of Enemy	**2 strands**
Nail Parings of Enemy	**3 pieces**

*Get a photograph of the person on whom you wish to place this curse; Put it in an incense burner or on a plain white saucer. Write the name of your enemy on a piece of pure parchment paper. Use only **Dove's Blood Ink** for this purpose. Allow to thoroughly dry and then sprinkle with seven drops of **Obeah Oil.** Carefully lay this directly on the photograph. Pour the previously blended mixture on the parchment. Now light the paper and allow everything to burn up. Concentrate on your enemy until the fire finally goes out. Let the ashes cool and then scatter them outside in the night air. Return to the house and carefully scrub your hands with heavily salted warm water. For additional hexing power, place a little of the first mixture in a **red flannel bag** or **chamois sack.** Sew the top tightly together and attach a **white cotton string.** Wear it around your neck for 7 full days. Then rip it off and toss it into the yard of your enemy.*

The above cursing charm was for many years a highly guarded secret of the mysterious Marie Laveau. It can be traced to a period in the early 1800's when this black woman reigned as Queen of all Voodoo in New Orleans and the surrounding areas. It is still in popular use today in that city, as well as many other areas throughout the nation.

In 1831, Marie is said to have used this charm with little discretion and it is reported that many people were subjected to its evil. One instance was a black house servant. He was a vocal nonbeliever in Voodoo. Yet while in apparently good health, he suddenly dropped dead on his way home from the market. This man's unexpected demise was widely believed to have been caused as a dire warning to others who might consider challenging the Laveau Voodoo power.

BLACK CURSE OF DEATH

Doctor Alexander's potent cursing charm can be prepared quite easily. It is to be undertaken only at midnight on a night when the moon is full. Take a piece of parchment paper and write the name of your enemy. Use only ***Dove's Blood Ink*** for this purpose. Place it in an ***incense burner or on a plain white saucer.*** Now carefully blend all of the following ingredients:

Rosemary (crushed)	**1 teaspoon**
Frankincense	**4 teaspoons**
Lavender Incense	**6 teaspoons**
Myrrh Incense	**2 teaspoons**
Orris Powder	**4 teaspoons**
Patchouly Leaves	**1 teaspoon**
Saltpeter	**1/2 teaspoon**
Sandalwood Incense	**6 teaspoons**
Cinnamon (crushed)	**1 teaspoon**

Take some ***Dragon's Blood Incense*** and draw a circle around your incense burner or plain white saucer. Lay ***1 piece of Lodestone*** in front of the burner or saucer. Pour a little of the above mixture into the burner and light. Concentrate on your enemy. Go to bed while it is still smoldering. Do this for 7 straight nights. Your enemy is then said to be destroyed. For even more hexing power, place a little of the mixture in a ***red flannel bag*** and sew the top tightly together. Toss the bag by the front door of your enemy's house.

This potent curse is credited to the Voodoo High Priest who practiced under the name of Doictor James Alexander, or simply Doc Alexander. He was the first Voodoo practitioner of any consequence to openly challenge the totalitarian rule of the prevailing Voodoo Queens. He was in direct competition with High Priestess Malvina Latour from about 1870 to sometime in the 1880's. Alexander was a tall, handsome mulatto from Mississippi who was three-fourths Indian and one-fourth Negro. He claimed to have been born "with a caul and a gift from God in my hands."

A SIMPLE WAY TO CURSE SOMEONE

Four Thieves Vinegar	**1/4 cup**
War Water	**9 drops**
John the Conqueror Incense	**7 tablespoons**
Peace Powder	**1 packet**

Take the ***Four Thieves Vinegar*** and put it in a bottle. Then write your enemy's name, 9 times, on a piece of ***clean parchment paper.*** Use only ***Dove's Blood Ink,*** *or* your own blood. Put this paper in the bottle with the vinegar and throw it in the moving water of a river or stream. This act is alleged to force your enemy to leave his home or other place of residence. Then take the ***War Water*** and sprinkle it in front of your adversary's house. You must not be seen doing this. Quickly return home and burn 1 tablespoon of ***John the Conqueror Incense,*** each day, for 7 successive days. Also sprinkle some ***Peace Powder*** on all 4 sides of your house and yard. Before retiring for the night, read aloud **Psalm 70** for encouragement.

Carefully follow the above instructions and you will always be able to control your enemies. They will be made powerless to harm you in return. There will no longer be malice from their lips or threats from their homes toward you or any of your loved ones.

Rosalie, a powerful quadroon Voodoo Queen in the 1850's is said to have developed the above ritual. She is the only High Priestess ever to become a serious threat to Marie Laveau's dictatorial rule. Queen Rosalie tried to dethrone Marie from her position of supremacy by accusing her of theft and then taking her to court. She lost the case and then suddenly and mysteriously disappeared on a dark rainy night. Never again did anyone see or hear of Rosalie.

2

To Overcome Illnesses

DISEASE CURE

The most celebrated arrangement of letters by which cures are effected is **ABRACADABRA.** Such a mystical grouping is said to have originated from Serenusj a noted scholar and physician of the second century. This talisman is still popularly used by those who believe in and practice Voodoo in America today. Each letter is to be written it the blood of the user, or with ***Dove's Blood Ink.*** It must be inscribed on ***a piece of parchment (or plain white paper)*** in the form of an inverted pyramid. Or it may be engraved on an amulet.

The belief in the fantastic powers of this unique word is prevalent among the Voodoos. This talisman is simply to be hung around the neck of any sick person. And it is thereby said to cure any disease. Carried in the pocket of one who is well is said to ward off illnesses. Such a talisman is claimed to cure everything from a bad toothache or bruises to epilepsy and insanity.

A B R A C A D A B R A
A B R A C A D A B R
A B R A C A D A B
A B R A C A D A
A B R A C A D
A B R A C A
A B R A C
A B R A
A B R
A B
A

ANOTHER GREAT SICKNESS CURE

A similar word to be used in the same manner as mentioned previously was developed in ancient times. This word is also said to act as a cure for disorders of every type. It too is extremely popular in American Voodoo today. Write ABRACALAM in the manner shown below. Use only the blood of a black cat or Dote's Blood *Ink* on parchment or plain white paper. It may also be engraved on an amulet. Hang it on a chain or string and wear around your neck.

A B R A C A L A M
A B R A C A L A
A B R A C A L
A B R A C A
A B R A C
A B R A
A B R
A B
A

DOCTOR JOHN'S BUG CURE CHARM

Find a ***live grasshopper, cockroach or bedbug.*** Pull off the legs. Carefully fold the insect into a small piece of ***unbaked biscuit dough***—place in your mouth and quickly swallow. This unusual charm is said to cure the chills, overcome a fever, and clear up a number of other ailments in a hurry. Never bake the dough before eating it or you will destroy the power of the charm. And the bug must still be alive when placed in the dough.

Doctor John, a Voodoo King from the 1820's to the 1880's is said to have devised this bug cure. He also worked under the names of Bayou John, Voudou John, John Montanet, Jean Montaigne, Jean Bayou and John Fecille. Doctor John claimed to have psychic powers and he was written up in *Harper's Weekly* of November 7, 1885. The article said: "He stated that he had a Master whom he was bound to obey; that he could read the will of his Master in the twinkling of the stars; and often on clear nights the neighbors used to watch him standing alone on some street corner staring at the welkin; pulling his woolly beard, and talking in an unknown language to some imaginary being."

DOCTOR YAH YAH'S VIOLET CHARM

Violets were said by Doctor Yah Yah to be a wonderful aid for avoiding or overcoming any illness or disease. These pretty purple flowers give off powerful healing vibrations. Place some ***violets*** in a ***red flannel bag***, tightly tie the top shut, and attach a ***white cotton string*** and wear around your neck for protection. Change the flowers in the bag every 7 weeks. For even more potency, sprinkle some crushed violets in each corner of every room in your home.

Doctor Yah Yah, sometimes known as Doctor Yah, appeared on the Voodoo scene in New Orleans during-the late 1850's. Specializing in healing and fortune telling, this unusual black man operated during the period when Doctor John was widely known as the "big Voodoo man" in that city. Doctor Yah Yah was a mere house slave while he practiced Voodoo, yet he became one of the most powerful and respected Kings. He was less well known than Doctor John but he still commanded a fantastically large following.

SNAKE CURE CHARM

This charm was long one of the secret methods Marie Laveau claimed to have successfully used in curing rheumatism.and similar ailments. Get a ***fresh rattlesnake skin*** and place it in a hot oven (450 degrees) to dry. Then allow it to cool and rub it thoroughly with grease which has been obtained by slowly boiling ***a whole black dog.*** Such grease is to be applied only during the dark of the moon. If a black dog isn't available, use grease obtained by stewing a black cat, black rooster, or a cow's hoof. A long and healthy life will be assured when the skin is worn around the waist, next to the body. It may also be tied on an arm or leg joint which aches—the pain is said to immediately stop.

Laveau's terrible rites and rituals were the talk of old New Orleans. Her control over blacks was dictatorial and absolute. She often danced with large numbers of snakes at her ceremonies, one of which was called "Zombi." One such service was colorfully described by the *New Orleans Times* in 1872: " . . . a box was brought up to the fire, from which was taken a black snake; he was cut in three pieces, one piece was put in by Marie Lavaux, one piece by the old man who put in the salt, and one piece by the young girl, who put in the pepper; then all joined in chorus of the same song: *'Mamzelle Marie chauffez ca'*; then the queen called for a 'cat,' it was brought, she cut its throat, and put in into the kettle."

MADAME AUGUSTE'S RHEUMATISM CURE

Buckeyes were often used by a High Priestess calling herself Madame Auguste. She claimed it to be a sure cure for rheumatism and other related diseases. Auguste simply wrapped ***a new one dollar bill*** around a ***buckeye,*** secured it with ***a rubber band or piece of string,*** and attached a length of ***plain white cotton string*** to it. This was then to be worn around the neck as a protective amulet. Or it could be carried in your *left* pocket. The end results were said to be the same. This mystical charm is also said to cure piles.

Madame Auguste was the first widely known and respected white Voodoo Queen in New Orleans. This tall and statuesque blonde beauty was initially heard of in the 1850's when she worked with Marie Laveau. Auguste started out as a sensuous dancer at Marie's rituals and she was an extremely popular orgy participant. Her fabulously proportioned body, flowing mane of golden hair, and Grecian face, attracted many wealthy and influential men to the ceremonies. Her reputation as a "wild and versatile degenerate lover" quickly spread throughout the city and crowds flocked to watch her and to partake of her generous amorous nature. Auguste was finally able to start her own Voodoo cult in 1869 when Laveau went into forced retirement. She lost one eye in later life and her natural beauty went down the drain. Madame Auguste became a horrible looking old crone and mysteriously disappeared in 1895.

3

To Control a Person Sexually

TO INDUCE ORAL SEX PLAY

This charm was specifically designed by the notorious Don Pedro to assist inhibited sexual partners. It is said to be especially good in bringing a hesitant female to willingly and enthusiastically participate in fellatio, or a restrained male to perform cunnilingus on his mate or lover. If each step is carefully carried out, one is said to obtain the ultimate enjoyment from partaking in this type of sexual activity. You will need all of the following ingredients:

Special Perfume No. 20	**1 bottle**
French Love Powder	**1 packet**
Blessed Pink Love Candle	**1**
Lucky John the Conqueror Incense	**1 box**
Vanilla Bean	**1 piece**

Now follow these directions carefully. Draw your bath **water** each morning for 7 successive days. When the tub is filled, add 10 drops of ***Special Perfume Oil No. 20.*** Get in and soak for 10 minutes, no longer, no less. Then climb out and thoroughly dry yourself off. Sprinkle some ***French Love Powder*** on your neck, bosom and genital area. Light the candle and allow it to burn for 1 full hour. While the candle flickers, stand before it.for 7 minutes, and concentrate on the person you sexually desire. The candle must begin the east corner of the room for maximum effectiveness. Also burn some of the ***Lucky John the Conqueror Incense.*** This is said to eliminate any forces working against your wishes. Carry the smoldering incense around the room so its smoke reaches every corner.

After all of these steps are properly carried out, place a ***Seal of Venus talisman*** in your purse or pocket. This combination will force others to desire you sexually even after you have lost them. You will absorb good vibrations and your love partners will meet your every sexual demand with a cheerful face. They will remain with you, and faithful, for so long as you wish. And they will happily perform in the bedroom in an attempt to totally satisfy your every sexual need.

Don Pedro was a powerful self-styled Voodoo King in New Orleans of the 1850-1890 period. In *New Orleans as it Was,* written in 1895, H.C. Castellanos refers to Don Pedro as "The Prince of the occult science." He then goes in to say: "Don Pedro is now the recognized head of the sect, and his adepts, I am told, are legion." Pedro, it seems, took over the Voodoo leadership in New Orleans from another powerful High Priest who was best known as Doctor John and whose peak of power was in the 1840's.

TO REMOVE OBSTACLES TO SEX

This Voodoo charm is to be used when you run into problems with the conquest of a potential sexual partner. It was one of Marie Laveau's favorite methods of inducing sexual relations. The charm is particularly good to try when someone you strongly desire keeps saying no. Start off by wearing absolutely no piece of black clothing. Complete nudity is preferable though. A girl must remove all pins from her hair. Then begin by filling a ***white china saucer*** with the following items:

Molasses	**3 tablespoons**
Quicksilver	**1 teaspoons**
White Sand	**7 tablespoons**

Place a ***Red & Blue Double Action Candle*** in the center of the saucer and light it. Kneel, make the sign of the cross, and pray for a successful encounter. Concentrate on the person you want to have relations with. Make a wish that all obstacles to a sexual conquest will be hastily removed.

Now begin to eat some previously prepared ***gumbo and rice.*** This must have been slowly cooked in a cast iron pot with a ***live snake.*** Write your own name and the name of your desired lover on ***2 separate pieces of parchment paper,*** using your own blood (if a female, use some menstrual blood). Drop both pieces of paper into a cup of burning whiskey. Light a ***seven Notched Red Candle.*** Leave the candle until 1 notch is burned. Burn 1 notch each day, for 6 additional days. Pray for success each time. You should reach your goal during this period of time.

Marie Laveau ruled supreme as Voodoo High Priestess in the city of New Orleans from the 1820's until she was forcibly dethroned by a large group of her peers on June 7th, 1869. She was then well over 70 years old and believed incapable of properly performing her rigorous duties as Queen of the Voodoos, She devoted her remaining years to being '"Spiritual Adviser" to condemned criminals in Parish Prison.

TO COMPLETELY CONTROL SOMEONE SEXUALLY

This talisman represents the spirit of *Erzulie,* a powerful Voodoo deity who helps the possessor to dominate and gain full sexual control over those of the opposite sex. ***Embroider in gold on red satin*** and carry with you. It may also be engraved on a ring or an amulet. ***Note:*** the heart denotes *Erzulie,* Voodoo goddess of home and purity. The penis stabbing the heart signifies the loa *Legba,* a phallic god of fertility. When these two powerful spirits join together, a union of sexuality is out of the control of the wearer. This talisman should be presented as a gift to anyone you wish to gain sexual power over. Your every fantasy will eventually be realized in a lovemaking encounter. Use this talisman with discretion for it is extremely potent. The cross and the halved circles add to the sensuality of the person who wears this talisman. *Erzulie* requires a sacrificial offering of ***2 white pigeons*** before she will take any action in your behalf. Her favorite days are Tuesday and Thursday.

THE POTENT CLOVE CHARM

This very old Voodoo charm is credited to High Priestess Sanite Dede. She said you must first arrange to meet with the person you desire sexually. When he or she arrives, place a ***clove*** in your mouth and suck lightly. This act is believed to soften their resistance against your amorous advances. Also take a ***glass of warm, sweetened rain water*** and toss it out the back door the moment your lover enters the front door of the house. Be sure to have your own back to the door when this is done or the spell will not work. Take another fresh piece of clove and proceed to suck on it. While the clove is still in your mouth, kiss the person. Touch your tongue to his or hers, whichever the case may be. This is said to help get what you want with no strings attached. If any resistance is still encountered, get a strand of his or her hair. Place it where a faucet can continously drip on it. Wear a ***Lodestone amulet*** on a ***gold chain*** around your neck. This type amulet will further induce the person towards making love with you.

Sanite Dede was the most feared name in New Orleans Voodoo circles between 1800 and the 1820's. She was an old quadroon who came from Santo Domingo as a free woman. This Voodoo Queen's power was at its peak in 1825 and she ruled with terror. Dede is the earliest recorded High Priestess of any notoriety in New Orleans history. Beginning her reign about the time of the Louisiana Purchase (1803) she was eventually succeeded by the famed Marie Laveau.

4

To Gain Gambling Luck

TO DISCOVER WAYS OF WINNING

This fantastic talisman helps one to discover secret means of winning in all forms of gambling. It insures the possession of a good hand of cards. And it aids in the selection of horses, etc. Embroider in ***gold silk on bright yellow satin*** and carry with you. It may also be engraved on a ring or an amulet. ***Note:*** the hand holding the candle aloft represents the loa *Gbo,* protector of anyone who gambles fairly. The presence of *Agarou Tonnerre is* again noted in the snake symbols. He is extremely evil and powerful and this spirit force will utilize his dangerous strength to protect the wearer from machinations of dishonest-people when playing cards, shooting craps, or taking part in any other games of chance. The power and wrath of both *Gbo* and *Agarou Tornnerre* will turn against the wearer of this talisman should he or she practice deceit while gambling. The other symbols are also important as they assist in directing the spirit forces. *Gbo* requires an offering of red wine, while *Agarou Tonnerre* demands a black rooster before they will take any action in your behalf.

A GAMBLING CHARM OF GREAT CONSEQUENCE

The following materials are to be placed in a ***red flannel bag or chamois sack,*** and then used according to the directions given by Doc Alexander.

Cinnamon	**1 teaspoon**
Dragon's Blood	**1 teaspoon**
Myrrh	**1/2 teaspoon**
Lodestone	**1**
Jamaica Ginger	**1/2 teaspoon**
Winner's Powder	**1/4 teaspoon**

Sew the top of the bag tightly together and attach ***a long piece of white cotton string.*** Anoint the bag with 9 drops of ***Winner's Circle Oil.*** Wear around your neck or carry in the left pocket whenever gambling or going to the races. This charm is said to help you to consistently win.

Doctor Alexander claimed to have used this charm for a great number of years. This man tried to pass himself off as a Mexican conjure expert and he had actually practiced Voodoo in Mississippi for many long years before finally arriving in New Orleans with his beautiful white wife, Clemence. His power was at its height in the 1870's. Alexander became very rich as a direct result of his Voodoo practice. He was a big property owner and wisely invested all of his money.

GOOD LUCK FOR GAMBLERS

The word ***Bedooh*** *is* to be carefully inscribed on rings, charms, or anything else carried on the person. The blade of a pen knife would be suitable as well. This word was adopted by modern Voodooists as a device to draw good fortune while gambling.

This unusual talisman was regularly sold by a Voodoo King named Bert Ellis who was a power in New Orléans of the 1930's and 1940'8. Doctor Ellis or Doc Bert was convicted of fraud in 1942 and sent to the penitentiary for a number of years. He had been accused of selling a white man a guaranteed cure for his son's epilepsy. The man paid Doc Ellis $150 for his supernatural charm and the son later became incurably insane as a direct result of the specific treatment.

KITTY BROWN'S WASHING CHARM

Get some ***Chewing John Root*** and boil it in 1 gallon of ***rain water.*** Allow it to cool and then bottle the liquid. When you intend to gamble, wash your hands in this tea-like brew. Carry a small piece of this same root in your pocket. Chew on it when selecting a card or placing a bet. This potent root, when properly used, is said to improve chances of winning money at all games of chance.

This was one of the most popular gambling charms of the 1920 period and is credited to Kitty Brown, a practicing Catholic and well known "Hoodoo Doctor." Brown was a squat, black, unexpressive old woman who hobbled around the streets of New Orleans peddling her Voodoo wares. She specialized in love, marriage and gambling charms. This woman was best known because she always grew her own herbs and supplied other Kings and Queens with roots, leaves, etc. Her fee for revenging a broken love affair started at $100 and went up from there. She did athriving business in her day.

DOCTOR SOL'S BUCKEYE CHARM

This unusual charm is said to act as a magnet in attracting money to anyone who gambles. Thoroughly blend the following ingredients:

Money Drawing Powder	**1 teaspoon**
Money Oil	**3 drops**

*When well mixed into a thick paste, rub it all over a piece of **Buckeye.** Then wrap the root in a **new one dollar bill** and place between **2 Brown Jumbo Candles.** Anoint each candle with the same paste mixture. Light 'the candles and let them both burn for 1 hour. Concentrate on winning money during this time. Then blowthe candles out from left to right. Pick up the wrapped root and place it in a **piece of red flannel.** Tie it tightly together with somethread and then wear it around your neck on a **white cotton string** or you may carry this wrapped root in your pocket whenever you are going to take part in any game of chance.*

This special charm is credited to a black Voodoo King of the 1870's and 1880's who successfully practiced under the name of Doctor Sol. His real name was Solomon Hastings add he had offices on Orleans Street in New Orleans. Papa Sol, as He was popularly called, worked with Doctor Alexander and a Queen named Annie Gould, a Negress of some stature in the Voodoo world. Doctor Sol was held in high esteem until his partner Alexander passed on. He then seemed almost immediately to lose his reputation as a sorcerer and conjure man.

MARIE LAVEAU'S SPECIAL GAMBLING CHARM

Get a ***whole nutmeg and drill a small hole*** in it. Then fill the opening with ***mercury*** and plug the end with ***white candle wax.*** Place the nutmeg in a ***red flannel bag or chamois sack*** and add the following ingredients:

Five Finger Grass	**1 piece**
Gold Magnetic Sand	**1/2 teaspoon**
John the Conqueror Root	**1 piece**
Lodestone	**1**
Lucky Hand	**1 piece**
Silver Magnetic Sand	**1/2 teaspoon**

Carefully sew the top of the bag shut with some ***white cotton thread.*** Anoint the bag with 7 drops of ***Special Perfume Oil No. 20.*** Attach a ***white cotton string*** to the bag and wear around the neck. Anoint the bag again every 7 days.

Marie Laveau is credited with creating this special "Gambling Charm," and she sold many thousands of them in her long and controversial lifetime. This lady of Voodoo, often thought to have been black, was actually a mixture of Negro, Indian and Caucasian. She succeeded Sanite Dede as High Priestess of Voodoo in the late 1820's and then ruled with an iron hand for approximately 40 years thereafter. Her feats are legendary and her influence is still felt today.

5

To Attract or Find a Mate

THE POWER OF BLUESTONE

Bluestone was a highly favored item in the Voodoo magic of High Priestess Regina Nicaud. It is said to accomplish wonders when properly used by a person in love. Carry one of these stones in a pocket or purse until you meet the person you would like to marry. Then take it out and hold it between your hands. When your eyes meet those of your true love, hastily rub your hands together. He or she will be unable to resist your marriage proposal. They are said to be forever in your bondage. Feelings of love and devotion will never wane.

Nicaud became deeply involved in Voodoo around the late 1850 period. She began her work as a sensual dancer and an eagerly willing sex orgy participant at Mama Antoine's house on Dumaine Street, where Antoine and Marie Laveau jointly presided over many meetings. Regina became a full Voodoo Queen in the 1870's.

MARIE SALOPPE'S CAKE OF LOVE

It is said to be rather easy to force a proposal at any given time from someone you love. Even a brand new acquaintance can be made to fall madly in love with you by utilizing this unusual method of conjuring. ***Pink Love Powder is*** to be used when a girl wants to snare a particular man. ***White Love Powder*** is to be used when a fellow desires to marry a certain female. Purchase some of this highly potent powder. Make any kind of a cake you prefer. When mixing the basic ingredients, blend in a pinch of the appropriate colored love powder. Bake in a moderate oven (350 degrees) and when finished, serve some of the cake to the person you wish to wed. If it is eaten and enjoyed, marriage will soon be suggested.

Marie Saloppe was an extremely powerful High Priestess of Voodoo immediately preceding Marie Laveau in the late 1820's. She was a most important queen, the one who forcibly pushed Sanite Dede out of the picture. This black lady was Laveau's instructor in the art of Voodoo worship. They first worked together and jointly presided over all ceremonies of- any consequence in and around New Orleans in the 1820's and 1830's.

TO FIND A SUITABLE PARTNER

This talisman gives the possessor the power to see through the intentions of others in regard to love and marriage. It enables one to see a prospective partner as they really are, not as they may pretend to be. Embroider in black silk on yellow satin and carry with you. It may also be engraved on a ring or amulet. ***Note:*** the smiling face represents the powerful goddess *Ezili-Freda.* She is the Voodoo- loa of beauty. The other symbols surrounding *Ezili-Freda* add to the fertility of the wearer and help to assure many healthy children and a blissful married life. It is always best to wear or carry this talisman from sunrise to sundown. Never take it off during these impor tent hours or the spell will be broken, And never let anyone see or touch it under any circumstances or suffer serious consequences' Ezili Freda requires an offering of any kind of perfume or some almond flavored water before she will take any action in your behalf.

THE ANCIENT FROG CHARM OF LOVE

When you truly desire a person, and would like to marry them, this ancient charm is said to work wonders. It was popular in Marie Laveau's early New Orleans Voodoo practice. Find a ***live frog*** and kill it with a sharp blow to the head. Put the frog in an ***ant bed*** and leave it there until all the flesh is eaten. Then thoroughly dry the bones in the sun or a hot oven. When completed, search among the bones until you find one in the shape of a fish hook, Pull it out and set it aside. Bury all the others where they cannot possibly be found by anyone.

Now arrange a date with the person you desire so strongly to win. When this fellow or girl is not looking, hook the frog bone firmly in any piece of their clothing. He or she will instantly feel a powerful surge of love for you. Marriage will immediately come to mind. Expect a hasty proposal. You will obtain a devoted lover and mate.

Marie Laveau used the above charm in many instances with a great deal of success during her long and terrifying reign as the New Orleans High Priestess of Voodoo. She paid heavily for police protection and was never really bothered by the law while plying her trade. Marie had fierce black eyes, was born a Roman Catholic, and even attended mass daily while ruling as supreme Queen of all Voodoo.

TO MAKE SOMEONE FALL IN LOVE

If you happen to meet a stranger, fall in love, and would like to get married, this old Voodoo charm of Marie Laveaus is said to do the job. It makes those of the opposite sex desire you more than life itself. A marriage proposal will be forthcoming. Thoroughly blend the following ingredients:

Black Musk Powder	**2 teaspoons**
Cassia Powder	**1 teaspoon**
Cassia Bark	**1 piece**
Myrrh Incense	**1/2 teaspoon**
Saltpeter	**1/2 teaspoon**
Sandalwood Incense	**2 teaspoons**

Place this mixture in a ***red flannel bag or a chamois sack*** and sew the top tightly together. Attach a ***white cotton string*** and wear it around your neck. Good results should be gained in approximately 1 month.

Marie Laveau, herself an expert in this sort of charm had a long string of lovers. She lived with a mulatto named Christophe Glapion who moved in with her soon after her husband mysteriously disappeared. This relationship lasted from 1822 to 1835 when he passed away under rather suspicious circumstances. Marie and Christophe had 15 children in rapid succession, one being a daughter who was also named Marie, born on February 2, 1827.

6

To Cast Love Spells

TO BE MORE APPEALING

This talisman endows the wearer with every virtue and talent. It stimulates others to look upon the owner as a good prospect for a torrid love affair or even marriage as a possibility. Embroider in ***silver on saffron colored satin*** and carry with you. It may also be engraved on a ring or an amulet. ***Note:*** the full moon and two partial 30 moons represent the loa *Lisa,* whose forces of love generate outwardly to all members of the opposite sex who appeal to the wearer of this talisman. *Lisa* works best during the evening hours, and especially on nights with a full moon. The other planetary symbols add much to the attraction power of *Lisa.* And the miscellaneous symbols help to direct her forces toward any person you concentrate upon. Try to get someone you desire to touch this talisman as the rays of the full moon bathe it. Deep and unending love is said to be the end result. *Lisa* requires an offering of menstrual blood before she will take any action on a woman's behalf, and semen before helping a man achieve his goal.

DON PEDRO'S CHARM OF LOVE

Parchment Paper	**7 pieces**
Blessed Pink Love Candle	**7**
Van Van Perfume Oil	**1 bottle**
Come to Me Powder	**1 package**
Special Perfume Oil No. 20	**1 bottle**

Take the pieces of parchment paper and write the name of your lover on each with some ***Dove's Blood Ink.*** Carefully place each piece of parchment under a separate ***Blessed Pink Love Candle*** and light all 7 candles. Allow the wax to drip down and completely cover the name on the paper. No one must be able to see the name. Then blow out the candles.

The next 15 days are crucial. After doing the above, proceed with the following daily ritual. Do not miss a day or you will have to start again from the beginning. Start by putting 3 drops of ***Van Van Perfume Oil*** in your daily bath water. Bathe immediately upon arising each morning. When finished and dried off, dust your neck and chest with ***Come to Me Powder*** and then get dressed. Sprinkle 3 drops of ***Special Perfume Oil No.* 20** on your outer clothing. Kneel before the 7 candles and light each, starting from the left and going toward the right. Allow them to burn for 15 minutes. Pray that your sexual charms will cause a loved one to think deeply of you. Do this and you will never be absent from his or her mind. The lover will be forced to come to you with desire in his or her eyes. Do not reproach or insult this person. Treat them with special kindness, smile a lot and be friendly. Do all of these things and the gods will smile upon your efforts. Your life will be full of beauty and sunshine.

This is another of Don Pedro's love specialties. He was a notorious Voodoo King in New Orleans of the 1850-1890 period. Pedro organized Voodoo ceremonies which turned out to be sexual orgies and charged a high fee to both whites and blacks who were invited to attend. One ritual, according to a reliable eyewitness, had the participants "engaged in one of the wildest orgies that the most prurient imagination can conceive. The women, having cast off their everyday apparel, had put on white camesoles—called today 'Mother Hubbards'—and were all found clad in this uniform attire. Blacks and whites were circling around promiscuously, writhing in muscular contraction, panting, raving and frothing at the mouth."

LOU JACKSON'S URINE CHARM

One of the most popular Voodoo love charms utilizes urine as one of its basic magical ingredients. Mix some of your own urine with the food being prepared for someone you desire to marry or have a sexual relationship with. Fix the meal just as you would any other. Invite your prospective partner or lover over to eat dinner. Serve them the food and you will immediately win his or her devoted love and admiration. A proposal of marriage or at least a proposition of a love affair will soon be forthcoming.

Lou Jackson, a notorious white Voodoo Queen of the 1870-1890 period, was said to have devised and used this unusual charm. She worked closely with Voodoo Doctor Alexander, ran a popular house of prostitution on Roman Street, and was one of this black man's many lovers. A great many Voodoo oriented interracial orgies were held at Lou's place of business. Lou Jackson was never held in high regard as a High Priestess in Voodoo circles. Many people believed she merely became involved in Voodoo as a means to increase her prostitution clientele.

ATTRACTION LOVE CHARM

An excellent love charm, credited to Marie Laveau, can easily be prepared by carefully mixing the following ingredients:

Archangel Herb	**1/2 teaspoon**
Lover's Incense	**1 teaspoon**
Yerba Buena (Spearmint)	**1 teaspoon**

Take a piece of ***pure parchment paper*** and write your prospective lover's name, 7 times. Use your own blood (females should use menstrual blood), or use ***Dove's Blood Ink.*** Place the parchment and the above blend of materials in an ***old tin can,*** light and allow to burn together. Collect the ashes and put them into a ***red flannel sack*** or a ***chamois bag.*** Tightly tie the top shut. Attach a ***white cotton string*** and wear around your neck. This charm will draw the one you love or sexually desire. He or she will be unable to resist making love to you, and marriage may be a possibility.

7

To Influence Others

TO HAVE INFLUENCE OVER THE OPPOSITE SEX

High Conquering Oil	**1 bottle**
CompellingPowder	**1 packet**
Cleopatra Oil	**1 bottle**
Lucky Blueing	**1 bottle**
Tonka Beans	**To suit**

Take a bath every day after adding 3 drops of ***High Conquering Oil*** to your bath water. When finished- bathing, rub your wrists, ankles, chest and throat with ***Compelling Powder.*** Then sprinkle yourself, all over, with ***Cleopatra Oil*** before leaving the house.

When laundering any of your clothing, always be sure to add 7 drops of ***Lucky Blueing*** to the wash water. In your dresser, put a ***Tonka Bean*** in each drawer used for holding clean clothing.

According to a Voodoo conjure man calling himself Professor Graham, if you do all of the above things properly, you cannot help but to gain power over friends of the opposite sex. Smile at all times and keep yourself attractive. Professor Graham was a Rampart Street Voodoo Doctor of the 1940's. He advertised openly, yet was able to avoid legal problems by simply not mentioning Voodoo. Graham felt.that his customers were all smart enough to read between the lines, and didn't have to be told it was Voodoo he was peddling.

TO INFLUENCE A LOVER

Magnetic Horseshoe	**1**
Magnetic Lodestone	**1**
Nutmeg of India	**1**
Seal of Good Luck	**1**

Take all of the above items and put them into a ***small red flannel bag or chamois sack.*** Never let anyone see or touch this charm bag or it will fail to work for you. Sprinkle the outside of the bag with 3 drops of ***Jockey Club Oil,*** once each week, and especially on the day you are going to be with your lover. Place it under your pillow just before he or she arrives. Then, before enjoying any form of sex play, sprinkle your hands with a little ***Drawing Powder*** and rub it in well. Follow these directions explicitly and you can induce your sex partner to do anything at your bidding. This charm is said to be especially good for bringing on oral sex play when your lover has hesitated or declined in the past.

This potent charm is believed to have been the brainchild of the extremely successful Rockford Lewis, who was widely known in New Orleans of the 1930's. This enterprising black man was born on a farm in Thibodeaux, Louisiana, in 1905. He first arrived in the city at the age of 15 and then 9 years later opened a drugstore on Royal Street which primarily marketed Voodoo merchandise.

TO GAIN INFLUENCE OVER ANYONE

This potent talisman gives the possessor the power to gain mental control over both friends and foes. It helps to change minds and makes others agree with the wearer. The talisman should neverbe taken off after it has once been placed around the neck, and the wearer should never be without it when around other people. Embroider in ***pink silk on bright red satin*** and carry it with you. It may also be engraved on a ring or art amulet.

Note: the fish in this talisman represents the Voodoo loa *Simalo* who feasts on eggs and human flesh. He is known to be a powerful cannibalistic spirit force who has a fantastic reputation for dependability and loyalty to those calling upon him for assistance. The other symbols are simply made to encase the power of *Simalo* and better direct his forces towards the person being influenced by the possessor of the talisman. Corn meal offerings are to be made to *Simalo* in order to stay in his favor, and to induce him to take appropriate action in your behalf. Failure to appease his appetite will result in a refusal to help.

8

To Break a Hex

TO OVERCOME A BAD SPELL

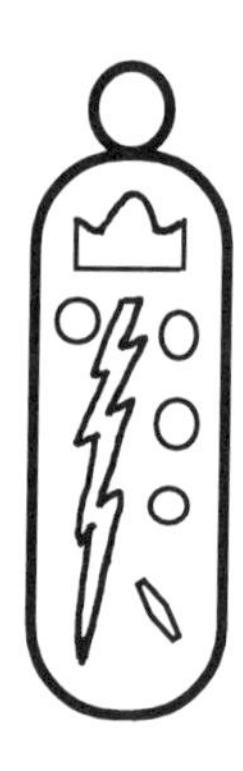

This fantastically powerful talisman can be used to break any kind of dangerous hex or curse. It breaks the power of any person who places a specific dastardly wanga (dreaded curse from Africa). And it offers unlimited protection to anyone who really has faith in the power of Voodoo. Embroider in ***white silk on black satin*** and carry it with you. It may also be engraved on a ring or an amulet. ***Note:*** the lightning in this talisman represents the Voodoo loa *Zaka*, commonly known as the peasant god. He is tremendously powerful and is believed to willingly assist anyone who gives him offerings of oil soaked bread, avocado slices and a glass of rum flavored with a variety of aromatic herbs. The other symbols are simply made to encase the power of *Zaka* and better direct it against the evil hex placed against the wearer of the talisman. Drums are played in honor of *Zaka* in order to stay in his favor; and to induce him to aid a believer.

STOP CURSES AND BREAK HEXES

Voodoo Doll	**1**
John the Conqueror Incense	**1 piece**
Seal of Maphistophilis	**1**

This spell breaking charm was said by Marie Laveau to be good only when you know the name of the person who is trying to cause the harm. If a doll is not available, simply cut a silhoutte of a human figure out of a piece of newspaper. It makes no difference how crudely the figure turns out. Now write the name of the person on the paper doll, or write it on a small piece of parchment paper and glue or pin it on a regular Voodoo doll.

Then, each day, snip off a piece of the doll, or tear off a small piece of the paper doll you have made. Slowly murmur the following invocation as each piece is burned:

> ***O curse placer, you are stopped, you are hampered by the great power of Damballah's spirit. Your hands are stilled, your legs become weak, your back aches. Your head is befuddled, your teeth chatter, and your loins quiver. O terrible one, release this sufferer or you must bear the most horrible consequences. Be damned!***

According to many Voodoo practitioners of note, the black spell will have been broken in from 5 to 15 days. Your enemy will have left you in peace and will turn his or her attention away from you; They may even move away, disappear, or be struck with a serious illness.

To guarantee that no other evil spell will be cast, Marie Laveau recommended burning ***John the Conqueror Incense*** daily, for 7 consecutive nights. This she believed would drive all evil spirits from the air around you and it also allows more friendly spirit forces into the home. Read **Psalm 7** as the incense burns. And carry the ***Seal of Mephistophilis*** with you at all times, for this is designed specifically for helping to conquer all enemies.

High Priestess Marie Laveau Charged from a minimum of $50 on up to $1000 to lift a curse, hex or bad spell from anyone. She was considered an expert in this type Voodoo practice as well as in all other phases of the mystical art. According to a report in the *New Orleans Times*, March 21, 1869, she conducted her last *service that month before being forced into retirement. The article described the females of the conclave as follows: ". . . their dresses were torn open, and each one conducted herself like a bacchante. Everyone was becoming drunk and intoxicated with the prevailing madness and excitement. As they danced in a circle, in the center of which stood a basket with a dozen hissing snakes whose heads were projecting from the cover, each* corybante *touched a serpent's head . . ."*

TO BREAK A CURSE OF AN EVIL EYE

Rosemary Oil	**7 drops**
Uncrossing Oil	**1 bottle**
Uncrossing Bath	**1 bottle**
Jinx Removing Bath	**1 bottle**
Uncrossing Powder	**1 packet**

Start your uncrossing ritual by putting the ***Rosemary Oil*** *in a glass of* ***rain water.*** *Stir in 9 drops of* ***Uncrossing Oil*** *and blend thoroughly. Set this in a window and leave it for 3 days. On the fourth day, sprinkle the water in all corners of your home. Do this only when alone for no one must be able to observe you doing it.*

Then bathe, each day for 7 consecutive days, in warm water to which 1 teaspoon of ***Uncrossing Bath*** *and 1 teaspoon of* ***Jinx Removing Bath*** *have been added. When finished bathing, dry off and then rub* ***Uncrossing Oil*** *all over your body. Sprinkle a little* ***Uncrossing Powder*** *in your socks and shoes.*

According to High Priestess Marie Comtesse, you must follow the above directions explicitly whenever you feel you have been burdened by a curse of the evil eye. Peace of mind will be yours. Love, goodwill, confidence and happiness will be drawn back into your life. Comtesse was a Voodoo Queen in the late 1800's and often went under the title of "La Comtesse." She was a big black woman, only 5'3" tall, but weighing well over 200 pounds. This powerful Voodoo figure was paid very well to bless homes and unhex people. She was well known in her day and feared by many.

9

To Gain Protection

EMILE LAILE'S SASSAFRAS CHARM

This bark was used quite extensively by Doctor Laile, a notorious New Orleans Voodoo practitioner in the early 1900's. Place the ***sassafras*** in a ***red flannel bag*** and sew the top tightly shut. Attach a ***white cotton string*** and wear around your neck. For further protection against illnesses or other dire things, boil some of this potent bark in fresh rain water. Bottle and save the strong tea. Add 1 teaspoon to a cup of boiling water and drink every 7 days or add 1 cup of this brew to your bath water every 7 days. Do all three of the above rituals and all evil is said to be overcome.

A SPECIAL PROTECTIVE TALISMAN

The word ***osy*** is commonly used as a Voodoo protective device. It is said to cause all enemies to stop bothering anyone who wears it. They are restrained from casting hexes against the person and can do them no physical harm. This simple word must be engraved on a ring or a pendulum. It may even be written on a piece of parchment paper, folded up, and carried in a pocket or purse. Only the owner's blood or Dove's Blood Ink may be used for this purpose.

This talisman is another invention of Doctor James Alexander who practiced Voodoo in the 1870-1880 period. He also had his offices on Orleans Street as did Emile Laile. Doctor Alexander often worked with two other notable Voodoo figures—Doctor Sol and ferocious Queen Ann, or Annie Gould, both blacks. Alexander's real *name was long believed to be Laurinsky Avery, but when he died, it was found by the police to be Charles La Fontaine. He was killed when a young boy in the neighborhood hit him in the head with a rock.*

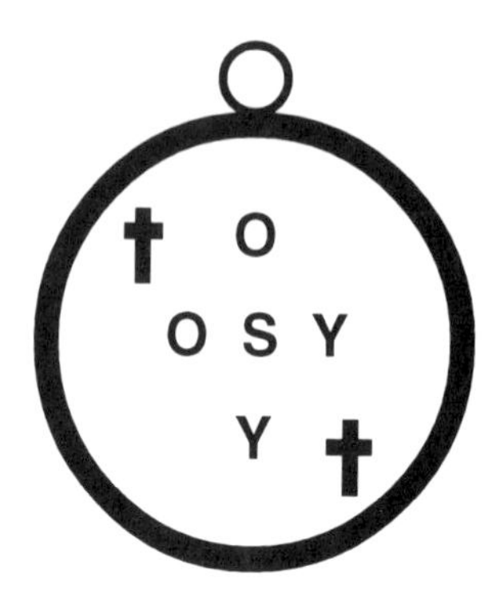

A POWERFUL HEALING SPELL

This is a rather complex healing charm, but it is well worth developing. It is said to have been one of Marie Laveau's most powerful Voodoo charms for overcoming and averting all types of illnesses as well as all harm from an enemy's hex. Get the following ingredients and put them in a neat pile:

Eucalyptus Leaves	**2 teaspoons**
Thyme Leaves	**2 teaspoons**
Winter's Bark	**1 cup**

Crush these materials until they are a fine powder and then bake in a hot over (450 degrees) for 15 minutes. Allow to cool and then add:

Cinnamon	**4 teaspoons**
MyrrhIncense	**2 teaspoons**
Frankincense Powder	**1/2 cup**
Orris Root Powder	**2 teaspoons**
Sage Powder	**1 teaspoon**
Saltpeter	**1 teaspoon**
Violet Powder	**4 teaspoons**

Mix all of these things together and place in a group of ***small red flannel bags or chamois sacks.*** Tie the tops together tightly and attach a ***white cotton string.*** Wear one of these bags around your neck. A little of this blend is to be poured out and burned in your house each day. When one bag is empty, wear another in its place. Do this consistently and no one in your house will ever become sick or be harmed in any other manner.

This charm was popularly prescribed by High Priestess Marie Laveau during her reign of terror from the late 1820's to 1869 in New Orleans. She was believed to possess great supernatural powers and was the first Voodoo Queen.to blend Catholicism with Voodoo. Her rituals often included worship of the Virgin Mary and various Catholic saints.

WILLIE LINK'S EUCALYPTUS CHARM

Leaves from this plant, or a piece of its root offer protection against colds and secret enemies. Simply stuff some of it into your pillow case, or slip some under the sheets. Never will you have to worry about catching a cold, or related illnesses. And you will be protected from the evil machinations of all who dislike you.

Willie Link was an enterprising black man who made his living by selling a variety of charm bags for $25 each. For those who couldn't afford the full price, he was kind enough to let them have it for $5.00 down and $5.00 each month until the bill was paid. Willie did quite well until he started marketing these same objects through the mail. He was then arrested and put out of business in 1925. Link received a prison term on a mail fraud charge. Nothing was ever heard of him again in the Voodoo world of New Orleans.

10

To Attract Good Spirits

TO DRAW THE FORCES OF GOOD

This is a special talisman designed to help its possessor achieve complete recovery from an illness, to gain assistance in any time of dire need, and to fully protect during moments of danger. It sets free the spirit forces which are able to overcome the immediate problem. Embroider in shaded silk on lilac satin and carry with you. It may also be engraved on a ring or an amulet. ***Note:*** the ugly, fanged-toothed man holding the bent wire configuration represents the Voodoo loa *Asiza*, god of all good magical power. Asiza is a friendly loa who aids the wearer of this talisman in every possible manner when a problem arises. He has the ability to call upon all other good spirit forces when necessary. The triangles surrounding Asiza all point toward the heavens which is believed to be the source of all good in Voodoo worship and practice. Asiza requires an offering of a live black snake before he will take any action in your behalf.

LUCKY NUMBERS DESIGNED TO ATTRACT GOOD SPIRITS

As with special days and times, Pastor J. V. Larson claimed everyone had certain numbers which attracted the forces of good to them. These long secret numbers of Voodoo are governed by the sign of astrology under which the person was born. Your special vibratory numbers are to be carefully written on a piece of parchment paper, using ***Black Cat's Blood*** *or* ***Dove's Blood Ink.*** *This parchment must be carried with you at all times without fail.*

TABLE OF NUMBERS

BIRTH SIGN AND DATE	FORTUNATE NUMBERS
Aquarius (Jan.21-Feb.19)	819 644 842 410 899 931
Pisces (Feb.20-Marcll 20)	513 216 800 319 539 713
Aries (March 21-April 19) .	106 791 41901253 959
Taurus (April 20-May 20)	119 452 721735 594 544
Gemini (May 21 - June 21)	545 483 601816 576 101
Cancer (June - July 21)	44 806 772 334 748 481
Leo (July 22-Aug.21)	452 317 222 90 398 555
Virgo (Aug.21-Sept.22)	706 558 200 329 901309
Libra (Sept.23-Oct.22)	491 172 500 507 871462
Scorpio (Oct.23-Nov.21)	810 177 563 641 21 825
Sagittarius (Nov.22-Dec.21)	521705 236 229 474 247
Capricorn (Dec.2-Jan.20)	211 357 191 170 545 907

Each morning, before the sun rises, and each evening before the sun sets, repeat **Psalm 4**, *three times. Try to keep your thoughts on a positive plane. The good spirits will continually remain close to you and offer a helping hand whenever necessary.*

Pastor J. V. Larson, a Voodoo High Priest in the early 1900's, ran the first official public Voodoo church. He was subsequently arrested and charged with embezzlement after stealing the funds of his sect in 1906. Larson immediately disappeared into thin air and nothing was ever heard of him from that time on.

TO GAIN FAVOR IN DIRE TIMES

John the Conqueror Incense	**1 packet**
Lucky Nine Mixture	**1 packet**
Seal of Knowledge	**1**

Keep some ***John the Conqueror Incense*** burning in your home at all times. Before going outside for any purpose, anoint your forehead with 9 drops of ***Lucky Nine Mixture.*** Wear a ***Seal of Knowledge*** upon going to bed or place it under your pillow and keep it there while you sleep. Then upon retiring for the evening, murmur the following invocation:

I am afraid and alone, or so I feel.
Fear I know, fear I know.
I am without heart, for weak am I.
I am down in the depths of darkness.
I need assistance, I need aid now.
Fear I know, fear I know.
Fear begone—fear begone—fear begone!
Yea the time has finally arrived.
Put strength, joy and gladness in my heart.
Lightness is the word, smile is the sword.
Let all fear flee from me.
Let me know no more fear, woe or doubt.
Fill my heart with hope and strength.
Fear begone—fear begone—fear begone!

This mystical ritual is credited to Mama Phemie who was widely known in 1920 New Orleans as a Voodoo Queen. She was a stooped and wrinkled old crone with one eyebrow higher than the other, and a large lax mouth. Her Voodoo work was conducted in a dirty little bottle-filled room with an open fire place. Mama's concoctions were always made by the flickering light of an old oil lamp as she believed it added to the charm's strength. Her smallpox scarred mulatto daughter, about 25 years old; assisted Mama Phemie in making all of her unusual supernatural mixtures.

11

To Overcome Legal Problems

TO INFLUENCE A JURY

Cascara Sagrada	1 oz.
Court Oil	1 dram
John the Conqueror Incense	1 packet
Success Candle	1
Calendula Flowers	7 oz.

Sprinkle 1 teaspoon of the ***Cascara Sagrada*** with the ***Court Oil*** and blend them thoroughly together. Put this mixture on a piece of ***clean white cloth or parchment paper.*** Fold the cloth or paper into a square and hide it under your mattress 7 full days before the trial. Leave it untouched. Then on the morning of the court appearance, pull the packet out from under your mattress, and set aside temporarily.

Now take some of the ***John the Conqueror Incense*** and mix it well with a pinch of ***Cascara Sagrada.*** Burn this on a lighted piece of pure ***Fast Lighting Charcoal.*** *As it* smolders, light the **Success Candle** and read **Psalm 7** aloud. Then hold the previously prepared packet over the candle and burn it completely.

Just before leaving for the courtroom, put the ***Calendula Flowers*** in your pocket or purse, whichever the case may be. It is said that the jury will be more inclined to be lenient.

This is another of Marie Laveau's long secret Voodoo spells. She has been credited with unbelievable success in dealing with all sorts of legal cases. Marie lived in an old unpainted shanty on Lake Pontchartrain during the 1830's. She later was to reside in a *comfortable cottage on St. Ann Street between Rampart and Burgundy, not far from Congo Square in New Orleans. Her yard was full of banana trees and bamboo plants, and the cottage itself was beautiful.'This residence, as well as a great sum of cash, was given her as a gift by a wealthy benefactor whose son's life she had saved at a rape trial. The boy was subsequently acquitted, and according to his father, it was Laveau's power that turned the tide and influenced the judge and jury. This St. Ann Street cottage is where Marie conducted much of her Voodoo business such as telling fortunes, selling charm bags (gris gris)and unhexing people. This same house was later lived in by her descendants until 1903 when it was finally torn down.*

TO WIN IN COURT EVERY TIME

This wonderful talisman aids its owner in overcoming all legal problems. If worn when appearing in court, it is said to guarantee the winning of any lawsuit. It offers protection against all injustice. Embroider in ***orange silk on blue satin*** and carry it with you. It may also be engraved on a ring or an amulet.

Note: the man with bugged-eyes and a long hooked nose represents the Voodoo loa *Atissou* who is well known for his legal knowledge and protecting qualities. He is said to strongly influence the thinking of a judge and jury. The other symbols are simply made to help direct his forces against all who try to do a legal injustice to the possessor. *Atissou's* loyalty can be better guaranteed if he is made an offering of a pair of sandals. He requires this before taking any action in your behalf.

Doctor Duke, a powerful Voodoo conjure man in the 1930's also read ***Psalm 35*** while waiting for trial. And if you happen to be on trial for murder, always read ***Psalm 22 and Psalm 35,*** daily, one after the other.

TO AVOID GOING TO COURT

Four Thieves Vinegar	**1/4 cup**
Black Candle	**1**
War Water	**1bottle**
John the Conqueror Incense	**1 packet**
Peace Powder	**1 packet**

Follow these explicit directions as given by Marie Leveau and you will be able to control your enemies and render them powerless against you in possible legal cases. You will have peace and comfort from foes. No tongue will have a sting against you and no legal threat will ever be carried out toward you or any loved ones.

Upon arising each morning, read ***Psalm 70*** for encouragement and mental peace. Then put the ***Four Thieves Vinegar*** in a bottle or jar. Write your enemy's name on ***parchment paper*** and put this in the bottle with the vinegar. Cork tightly, take it out of the house, and toss into the moving water of a river.or stream. This is believed to draw the person with it and force them to move away from you.

Then return home and burn the ***Black Candle.*** Pick up the melted wax after it hardens. Wait 3 days and then toss this wax in front of your enemy's house. Wait 3 more days. On the third night, take the ***War Water*** and sprinkle some of it in front of the same house. Immediately return home again and burn a little of the ***John the Conqueror Incense.*** Sprinkle the outside of your house, on all 4 corners, with ***Peace Powder.***

High Priestess Marie Laveau was the originator of this method for avoiding legal complications. She was considered to be an authority in this area of Voodoo as well as in most others. One of New Orleans noted attorneys worked for her. He gave Marie free legal assistance and advice in exchange for her Voodoo spells and aid. Marie was seldom hauled into court, but when she was, she never lost a case. In fact, this remarkable woman was often charged with fraud, but her cases never seemed to reach the courtroom.

12

To Attract Good Luck

TO DRAW AND HOLD GOOD FORTUNE

This special talisman attracts good luck in all forms to anyone who wears it. It is especially good for those who take part in any lottery for the talisman helps to draw a winning selection. And it should be worn or carried by anyone suffering with misfortune. Embroider in ***gold and silver silk on cherry-red satin*** *and carry it with you. It may also be engraved on a ring or an amulet.* ***Note:*** *the hand holding the knife upright represents the Voodoo loa Loco Attiso, god of luck and extreme good fortune. Loco Attiso is also known as a healer in times of sickness and will protect the owner against all forms of evil. The combination of the 1 large and 4 smaller triangles is said to concentrate the power of this spirit force and bring forth her strength instantaneously. Loco Attiso requires an offering of a plucked live chicken before she will take any action in your behalf.*

A POWERFUL GOOD-LUCK SPELL OF JOSEPHINE BAYOU

Wood Betony	4 teaspoons
Frankincense	1/2 cup
Orris Root Powder	2 teaspoons
Saltpeter	1/2 teaspoon
Vanillan Powder	4 teaspoons
Sandalwood Powder	1-1/4 cup

Blend all of the above ingredients in a large clean wooden bowl and cover tightly after each time it is used. A small amount (about 1 teaspoon) is to be burned every morning at sun-up and every evening as the sun goes down. This alone attracts good luck to your residence. But it must be done without fail on a daily basis.

Then to further attract good fortune to yourself, especially during times of extreme duress, the following items are required in addition to those given above:

Bend Over Oil	1 bottle
Seven Power Candle	1
Luv Luv Oil	1 bottle
Zodiac Oil (your sign)	1 bottle

First take 7 drops of ***Bend Over Oil*** and use it to carefully anoint the ***Seven Power Candle.*** Light the candle and leave it to burn until it goes out by itself. Before leaving your home, sprinkle a little ***Luv Luv Oil*** on your clothing. Then rub some ***Zodiac Oil*** on your ear lobes, behind the knees, and between each finger.

This charm is attributed to a black Voodoo practitioner named Josephine Bayou, who was widely-known during the late 1850 period in New Orleans. She never was recognized as a full-fledged High Priestess but was believed to possess abundant supernatural power. Josephine claimed she worked only as a "Good Voodoo." She performed hex breaking ceremonies and prepared special love and good luck charms.

TO ATTRACT GOOD FORTUNE TO YOUR HOME

*This wonderful old Voodoo charm of Marie Laveau is one of the best around and easiest to put into force. It is said to bring forth the favorable spirits of happiness and joy, not just to yourself, but to your entire household. What is known as the **"Secret Square of Voodoo"** is the key to properly casting this protective good luck spell. Take a square piece of **parchment paper,** any size, and fill in with numbers as directed below. Use only **Dove's Blood Ink,** or a little of your own blood, for this purpose. Be most careful to begin with the number 1 and end with number 16 or the charm will be powerless. As you make this charm, chant:*

O Voodoo spirits of lightness,
bless this house and all who reside in it!

4	9	2	14
3	5	16	10
7	12	13	6
11	1	8	15

Upon completion of writing in the numbers, turn the parchment paper over, and on the back, draw a simple outline of your house, enclose it with 3 circles, each drawn clockwise, and beginning with the outermost circle. Repeat the above invocation as you slowly draw each circle. This is what it should look like when finished:

New Orleans's mightiest Voodoo queen claimed fantastic results when she performed the above ritual. She is said to have obtained the secret from Doctor John in her early Voodoo days of the 1820's. Leaveau became a High Priestess herself in 1830. She started out by ruthlessly eliminating all rival Queens by hexes,

threats of violence, and even brutal beatings. Her competitors were either forced to leave New Orleans, or to work as secondary Queens under Marie's dictatorial guidance. Few disputed her authority and those who did seldom lived to tell about it.

13

To Induce Passion

TO STIMULATE SOMEONE

Brazil Wood was popular in Sanite Dede's Voodoo love magic. It is said to make a female quiver with desire and it makes an impotent man gain an immediate erection. A piece of this root is to be chewed in an effort to soften the heart of any person you sexually desire. It can be steeped into a delicious tea and sipped by a man incapable of satisfactorily performing the sex act. His organ will rise and become more rigid than it did in his more youthful years. A woman sipping this tea is said to easily overcome frigidity and all inhibitions. Carry this root charm in a pocket or a purse as a ready aphrodisiac.

Sanite Dede often worked closely with a Voodoo King by the name of Zozo, a herbal specialist and healer of some note. One of their joint sexual rituals was witnessed by a 15 year old boy in 1825. He had been taken to the ceremony by a slave woman owned by his father. In his own words: "Up sprang a magnificent specimen of human flesh—Ajona a lithe, tall, black woman, with a body waving and undulating like Zozo's snake. . . . Gradually the undulating motion was imparted to her body from the ankles to the hips. Then she tore the white handkerchief from her forehead. This was the signal, for the whole assembly sprang forward and entered the dance...."

MARIE SALOPPE'S SPECIAL DRINK

*Get some **Coriander Seeds** and add them to **1 quart of warm wine.** Let it sit for 7 full days and then give a little of it to someone of the opposite sex. They will become sensual and unable to leave you alone. This is said to be a wonderful aphrodisiac, often used by Queen Marie Saloppe, a woman who gained most of her Voodoo fame in the 1820's. Marie Laveau, a friend and confidant, eventually hexed Saloppe and then forced her out of the cult's leadership.*

This black High Priestess named a friend's child at birth and then blessed the little one in a special ritual. This child, Eliza, later became a much feared, blood-drinking Voodoo Queen during the 1870's. She credited Saloppe for her great power.

TO INCITE LUST

*This potent-talisman attracts passionate love from those of the opposite sex, even against their will. Total compliance with your sexual needs is said to be guaranteed. It is especially potent when your prospective sexual partner thwarts your initial advances. Embroider in **silver silk on black satin** and carry it with you. It may also be engraved on a ring or an amulet.*

The sun encased in a triangle represents the Voodoo loa Mystere, who is well known for her ability to warm the blood of even the most frigid or straight-laced lover. The snake beneath the triangle denotes the lea Aida Hwedo, wife of the lea Damballah. Aida Hwedo is a goddess who **loves** *fellatio and cunnilingus and she will induce your partner to freely participate in this type of sex-play after*

Mystere does her job of building up passion. An offering of 1 teaspoon peppered apple juice must be given to *Mystere* before she will take any positive action in your behalf.

WHEN SHYNESS STOPS YOU

This charm, according to Marie Laveau, is excellent when sexual conquests are stymied either through your own shyness, or by the bashful feelings of a potential partner. Simply take a ***live frog*** and boil it for 10 minutes. Then place the frog in a oven and bake slowly until it completely dries out. Allow to cool and then wrap it tightly in a ***black snake skin.*** Roll this combination up in a ***kerosene-soaked piece of red flannel.*** Sew tightly together at both the top and the bottom. Tie a long piece of ***white cotton string*** to this and wear around your neck when visiting your loved one. This is said to force a prospect to rid themselves of shyness. And they willingly throw themselves into sexual abandonment while in your embrace. Expect every kind of love play when using this charm

Marie Laveau had a great many charms and amulets which she used and guaranteed. All of her magical Voodoo items were said to achieve the desired end result. She was born in New Orleans about 1796 and was married on August 4, 1819, to Jacques Paris, another mulatto, and a carpenter by trade. Marie was in her early twenties at that.time and not yet involved in Voodoo practice. Her husband's death was mysteriously recorded as being in 1826, but he had actually disappeared shortly after their marriage. Laveau had long been calling herself "Widow Paris" before this supposed official death notice.

TO SEXUALLY ENSLAVE SOMEONE

Attraction Oil	**1 bottle**
Luv Luv Oil	**1 bottle**
Spikenard Powder	**1 packet**

Get an intimate picture (preferably a nude one) of the man or woman you wish to sexually enslave. Lay it face up on a piece of ***parchment paper.*** Sprinkle with 7 drops of ***Attraetion Oil,*** 7 drops of ***Luv Luv Oil*** and a little ***Spikenard Powder.*** Wrap the picture up in the parchment paper and place it all in a ***brown paper bag.*** Tie the top of the bag and bury it in your backyard by the door. Urinate on the freshly turned dirt. The burial spot must again be urinated on every seventh day. Also sprinkle this spotwith 7 drops of ***Attraction Oil*** every time you urinate on it. The person you desire will be under your domination so long as you continue anointing this buried charm.

This charm was an old favorite of Voodoo King Don Pedro who worked his popular trade in New Orleans from about the 1850's to the 1890's. This man was well known as a love specialist, and, though extremely powerful, was always in some kind of trouble with the law. Castellanos, writing in 1895, said: "The police have however, nearly broken up his business, having compelled him to go into hiding. He is heard of sometimes through the medium of the press, as he advertises occasionally as a healing medium. The organization of the Voudous, as an organization, has been suppressed in great measure by the efforts of our municipal authorities."

14

To Avoid Injuries

TO AVERT PHYSICAL HARM

This unusual talisman helps the wearer to avoid all types of physical harm and serious injury. Anyone who possesses such a talisman will never suffer injuries in the home or on a job. It is espesially potent when taken on trips away from familiar surroundings. Embroider in ***yellow silk on green satin*** and carry it with you. It may also be engraved on a ring or an amulet. ***Note:*** the circle with a dot in the center of the triangle represents the Voodoo loa *Gran Siligbo* who is a friendly and protective spirit force. He offers his services to anyone who believes in him and who will wear or carry one of these special talismans. The other symbols are simply made to keep his power close to the talisman's possessor. *Grim Siligbo* likes a simple offering of a spool of black thread before he will take any action in your behalf. Seldom will this loa ever fail the person who truly has faith in him.

SPECIAL CHARM TO HELP AVOID INJURIES

Sandalwood Incense	**1 teaspoon**
Mystic Rites Incense	**1 teaspoon**
Meditation Incense	**2 teaspoons**
Lavender Incense	**1 teaspoon**
Tobacco	**2 teaspoons**
Anise Seed (crushed)	**1 teaspoon**
Saltpeter	**1/2 teaspoon**
Myrtle Powder	**1 teaspoon**

Thoroughly blend all of the above ingredients in a small wooden bowl, cover, and set aside in a dark place until needed. A little is to be burned every evening as you meditate just before going to bed. This charm is said to allow you to visualize all danger areas in your life, and thereby helps you to foresee potential injuries before they actually happen to you.

This charm is a wonderful aid to those who feel they are under the influence of a bad spell or curse. It was used by Marie Comtesse, who was well known for her Voodoo power in New Orleans of the late 1800's. Marie was a very hefty woman with prominent "moon eyes." She was married to a handsome mulatto and gave birth to 2 daughters, both of which she claimed were virgin births. Comtesse always wore a long purple sarong-like dress and a red head band while conducting her Voodoo rituals. This High Priestess specialized in hex breaking and always attracted large crowds to her ceremonies.

TO PROTECT AGAINST INJURY

Blessing Incense	**2 tablespoons**
Orris Powder	**1 tablespoon**
Jalop Powder	**1 tablespoon**
Rosemary Leaves Redin	**1 oz.**
Dragon's Blood Leaf	**1/2 tablespoon**
Cascara Sagrada (crushed)	**1 teaspoon**

Thoroughly blend the above ingredients in a small bowl. Keep it tightly covered and stored in a dark corner when not in use. Burn a little of this mixture each evening just after sundown, for 9 consecutive nights. Then read ***Psalm 15*** upon going to bed. According to Octave Labeau, you can increase your protection against injuries by also placing a little ***Irish Moss*** under your bed, or under the rugs in each room of your home. Labeau claimed to be a great aunt of Marie Laveau and she worked as a lesser Queen under Marie during the 1850's. Octave Labeau, Miss Jackson and Leon Janipier were all well known names in New Orleans Voodoo; yet everyone of them were under the leadership and control of High priestess Marie Laveau.

SEVEN SISTERS' TOAD CHARM

This old charm was one of many used by Seven Sisters, a powerful conjure woman of the 1930's. Take a ***live toad or frog*** and burn it to ashes. Allow to cool and then gather up the ashes: Place them in a ***red silk bag.*** Sew the top tightly together with ***red silk thread.*** Attach a red silk thread and wear this charm around your neck It is said to relieve all aches and pains, and to protect the wearer from injuries.

Seven Sisters real name was Ida Carter. She was well known for her Voodoo conjuring in Alabama. This old black woman claimed to have started her magic work at the tender age of only 7 years because of her unlimited clairvoyant powers. She lived in Hogansville and operated out of a clean little white house which was trimmed in green.

15

To Stop Jealousy

TO OVERCOME YOUR OWN JEALOUS FEELINGS

Marie Laveau used this charm to aid others in successfully overcoming pangs of jealousy. Carefully follow these directions. First, gather together all of the listed ingredients:

Van Van Floor Wash	**1 bottle**
Patchouly	**1 packet**
Mystic Rites Incense	**1 teaspoon**
Powdered Peace Incense	**2 teaspoons**

First scrub the floor of the room you are going to use for casting the spell. Then go over it a second time with the Van Van Floor Wash. Let this dry well and then sprinkle the Patchouly on the floor in a 7 foot circle. Blend the ***Mystic Rites Incense*** and the ***Powdered Peace Incense*** and put them in an incense burner or on a plain white dish. Place this incense at the inside of the East edge of the circle and light it. Stand in the center of the circle and face the smoldering incense. Raise both arms above your head at about 45 degrees. Hold both palms facing the incense. Repeat the following invocation aloud, 3 times:

> ***O spirit of jealous healing, come to my assistance! I call upon you in the sacred name of Tetragrammation! Help me now in overcoming all feelings of jealousy and leave me without feelings of despair in the name of all good Voodoo gods!***

This spell must be cast for 3 consecutive nights, after sundown, and preferably at the stroke of midnight. If the instructions are properly carried out, all jealous pangs are said to disappear at the end of the ritual.

High Priestess Marie Laveau was notorious in her day for the multitude of sex orgies she organized for white men who wanted to make love to black or mulatto women. And she was equally as well known for her following of beautiful white society belles who desired sexual relationships with generously endowed black men. Some charges relating to such activities were brought against her over the years yet none ever went into court. Marie used blackmail and bribery to keep the law in her bondage. Her power was once so great that she was considered to be "untouchable" by the authorities.

TO OVERCOME JEALOUSY IN OTHERS

This potent talisman will overcome all feelings of jealousy in both the wearer and someone he or she loves. Its power helps to make love more serene. If a lover or mate feels pangs of jealousy, the power of this talisman will quickly suppress it. Embroider in ***blue silk on orange satin*** *and carry with you. It may also be engraved on a ring or an amulet.*

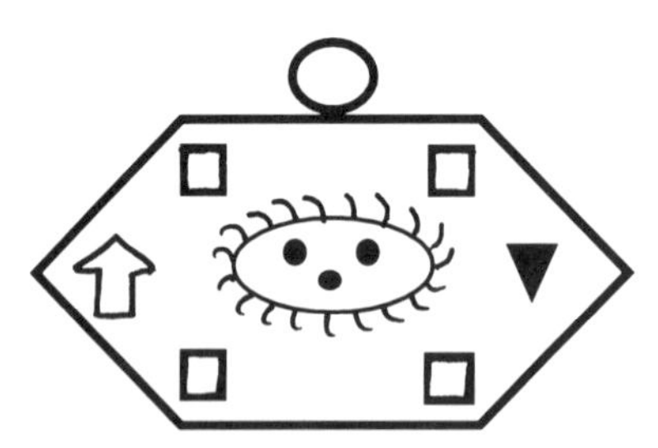

Note: *the spider in the above talisman represents the Voodoo loa Gran Zaraignee who has the power to eliminate envy from the heart of either sex. The other symbols are simply made to contain his spirit forces and to help direct them as needed. Anyone who becomes possessed of the spirit of Gran Zaraignee will be seen to crawl like a spider and to imitate a spider's movements. This loa is basically good and requires an offering of dried beans on a small white plate. This must be done before he will take any action on your behalf.*

TO PREVENT JEALOUSY IN A LOVER

Rose Buds	1/3 cup
Saltpeter	1/2 teaspoon
Orris Root Powder	1 teaspoon
Lavender Incense	1 teaspoon
Vanillan Powder	1 teaspoon
Bayberry Powder	1/2 teaspoon
Anise Seed (crushed)	1 teaspoon
Dragon's Blood Resin	1 teaspoon
Attraction Incense	1 teaspoon

Blend all of the above ingredients in a large wooden bowl. Tightly cover and set aside until needed. The following items are also necessary:

Fast Lighting Charcoal	1 oz.
Pink Seven Day Candle	1
Parchment Paper	1 piece
Luv Luv Oil	1 bottle

First you must sprinkle some of the special incense mixture on the ***Fast Lighting Charcoal,*** which has already started burning. Then light your ***Pink Seven Day Candle.*** Take the parchment paper and write the name of your lover on it, 7 times, with ***Dove's Blood Ink.*** Place this paper under the candle and leave it alone. It must not be disturbed and the candle must be allowed to burn itself out.

A little of the incense mixture must be burned at least once each day, but without fail just before going to bed at night. And you must sprinkle your body with a few drops of ***Luv, Luv, Luv Oil*** each morning upon arising for the duration of the time in which the incense lasts.

This spell, according to white Voodoo Queen: Lou Jackson, must be initiated each time a lover or mate shows any signs of envy and jealousy. It is said to immediately halt such destructive feelings. Lou Jackson's claim of being a legitimate Voodoo Queen in old New Orleans is felt to be dubious in some quarters. She was a prostitute and procurer for many years, and she even operated her own house of ill repute. Voodoo services were often held at her place and they were often raided by the police department.

16

To Prevent Losses

TO AVOID LOSING ANYTHING

This wonderful talisman prevents its possessor from suffering even the most minor of losses. And it also helps to find anything which was lost in the past. The talisman is designed to protect against financial losses, a loss of a lover, and especially natural calamities such as floods, earthquakes, hurricanes, etc. Embroider in ***dark brown silk on tan satin*** and carry with you. It may also be engraved on a ring or amulet.

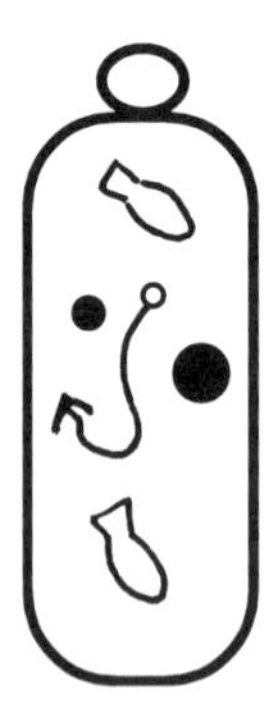

The fish hook in the above talisman represents the Voodoo Loa Ossange, protector of those people who are unfortunate enough to lose things. The other symbols are simply made to direct his powers when a search is being made, or when a calamity strikes the possessor. Ossange requires an offering of one boiled sweet potato, some roasted peanuts and a bottle of rum before his forces are unleashed. He will otherwise refuse to take appropriate action in behalf of the talisman wearer.

TO PROTECT YOURSELF AGAINST BEING ROBBED

This charm was especially designed by a Doctor Koku to protect a home, business or an individual from being robbed. It is said to stop all forms of thievery. You will need the following ingredients:

Sandalwood Incense	**1/2 cup**
Myrrh Incense	**1/2 cup**
Winters Bark (crushed)	**1/4 cup**
Vertivert Powder	**1/3 cup**
Lavender Incense	**1-1/2 cups**
Cinnamon Powder	**1/4 cup**
Frankincense Powder	**1/2 oz.**
Cloves Powder	**1/4 cup**

Blend all of the above ingredients in a large wooden bowl. They must be thoroughly mixed together in order to gain the full protective benefit of this fantastically powerful vibratory charm. A teaspoon of Saltpeter can be added if you desire for it is said, by some Voodooists, to make the spell even stronger. But this isn't a necessity!

Burn 1 teaspoon of this mixture each morning upon arising. Carry a little of it with you in a tightly closed sack. This sack or bag should always be on your person when you leave the house for any reason.

Doctor Koku first surfaced in 1902 New Orleans and claimed to have come directly from the Congo with a special God given Voodoo power. He rented a small cottage on St. Ann Street near Marie Laveau's old place. Koku didn't get much newspaper publicity and never could seem to attract a large following. No one really seemed to take him very seriously and he subsequently disappeared.

TO STOP THE LOSS OF A LOVER

Couch Grass	**1 teaspoon**
Luv Luv Oil	**1 bottle**
Love Powder	**1 packet**
Love Anointing Oil	**1 bottle**
Red Seven Day Candle	**1**

First take the highly potent ***Couch Grass*** and sprinkle it under your bed, on the mattress and under your pillows. Then upon arising each morning, rub a little ***Luv Luu Oil*** close to the most intimate parts of your body. Sprinkle a little ***Love Powder*** in the hair of your genital region.

Now take the ***Love Oil*** and rub down the ***Red Seven Day Candle.*** Write the name of your lover on a ***piece of parchment paper.*** Use only ***Dove's Blood Ink*** or some of your own blood for this purpose (a woman should use menstrual blood if possible). Place the paper on a plain white dish and set the candle on it. Light the candle and allow it to burn as you dress in preparation for the day ahead. Extinguish the candle upon leaving the room.

According to Doctor Jack, this exact same procedure must be followed religiously every morning for as long as there is any danger of losing your lover. It is said that he or she will be unable to leave you so long as the ritual is continued faithfully.

Doctor Jack was noted for his work as a Voodoo King in New Orleans of the 1850's and 1860's. He took over the large following of Doctor Yah Yah in 1861, when Yah Yah was arrested and exiled to spend the rest of his days as a plantation slave. Doctor Jack was especially famous for his love potions and sex charms.

TO FIND A LOST ARTICLE OF VALUE

Anise Seed (crushed)	**2 teaspoons**
Fast Luck Incense	**1/2 cup**
Four Leaf Clover Powder	**1 teaspoon**
Orange Seven Day Candle	**1**

Blend the first 3 ingredients in a wooden mixing bowl, cover tightly, and set aside in a cool, dark place until needed. Then at sundown, take a piece of ***clean parchment paper,*** and write upon it the name of whatever it is you have lost. Use only ***Dove's Blood Ink*** for this purpose or the charm will not take effect. Put the parchment on a clean white saucer, set the ***Orange Seven Day Candle*** over it, and light the candle.

Now put a piece of ***Fast Lighting Charcoal*** in a plain white dish or in an incense burner, and light it. Pour a little of the previously prepared incense mixture on this charcoal. As the incense smolders, recite aloud ***Psalm 57.*** This entire ritual must be repeated without fail, each day at sundown for **9 consecutive evenings,** or the spell will be broken. If you do each step faithfully you are said to find whatever has been lost at the end of the ninth day, if not before.

This charm was developed by Luke Turner who surfaced in New Orleans as a "Hoodoo Doctor" sometime during the 1930's. He claimed to be a nephew of Marie Laveau and, as a result of this, became very popular in Voodoo circles. This highly regarded conjure man had a toothless grin and always appeared to be totally confident of his mystical powers. Doctor Luke or Doctor Turner said he never placed death hexes, but instead used Voodoo only to assist others. He specialized in love charms which required genital hairs from a virgin as an important part of the ingredients. He was considered infallible when it came to constructing charms and amulets designed to aid in finding lost things.

17

To Influence Fate

TO ASK THE SPIRITS OF THE DEAD FOR ASSISTANCE

Frankincense Incense	1/2 oz.
Sandalwood Incense	3/4 cup
Musk Powder	1/2 cup
Wormwood (crushed)	1/4 cup
Wood Betony (crushed)	2 cups
Allspice	1/4 cup
Vetivert Powder	1/4 cup
Tobacco	1 teaspoon
Saltpeter	1/2 teaspoon
Verbena Leaves (crushed)	1 teaspoon
Solomon's Seal Powder	2 teaspoons

Doctor Alexander blended all of the above ingredients in a large bowl, covered the bowl tightly, and set it in a cool dark place until he was ready to use it. Here is what you must do:

Wait until midnight and then place 13 teaspoons of this potent mixture in 13 small mounds on a dark dish—black is preferred if at all possible. Light the mounds, starting with the one furthest from you, and proceeding in a counter-clockwise direction. As the smoke rises, take a ***Black Double Action Candle*** and place it in the center of the dish. Light the candle, and as it burns, call on the spirits of the dead for assistance in influencing your future fate. This entire procedure must always be undertaken in a serious manner for the mere dabbler will accomplish absolutely nothing.

Then take some more of the ***Solomon's Seal Powder*** and sprinkle a small amount in each corner of every room of your residence, or wherever the ritual is being performed. When finished with this step, carefully rub each door knob with ***Exorcism Oil.*** At this point it is too late to turn back. The ritual must be completed or the wrath of the dead will come down upon your head in all its fury.

At midnight, each night thereafter, burn 9 more mounds of the special incense mixture. The working of this and other ritualistic charms were undertaken in large groups under the "divine guidance" of Doctor Alexander. When done in a group, it always ended with an orgy. His beautiful blonde wife, Clemence, was also a highly regarded "Voodoo woman" in New Orleans between 1870 and 1880. She was a more than willing participant in all of her husband's Voodoo rites and ceremonies. She was said to have once been the most popular female at many orgies and was designated by her husband to be a special instructor of young females in the art of fellatio and sexual intercourse.

TO ENCOURAGE VISIONS OF YOUR FUTURE

Cinnamon Powder	**1 teaspoon**
Voodoo Incense Powder	**1/2 cup**
Sandalwood Incense Powder	**1/2 cup**
Aloes Powder	**1/2 teaspoon**
Dragon Blood Powder	**1/2 teaspoon**
Benzoin Powder	**1 teaspoon**

Blend the above ingredients in a small wooden bowl, cover tightly, and set aside in a cool dark corner of a closet. Burn a little of this mixture each night when the sun goes down, or just before retiring for the evening. Also sprinkle a little of it on the floor around your bed. This charm is said, by Marie Laveau, to make you have prophetic dreams and to have visions during waking hours. It may help to carry some of this blend around with you. Laveau used to put a little of it in a ***red flannel sack*** with 12 drops of ***Zodiac Oil.***

TO GAIN INSIGHT INTO THE UNKNOWN

This talisman brings clairvoyant powers to anyone who wears it while in trouble or in need of assistance. It reveals the most hidden secrets of the universe. And it enables the wearer to penetrate anywhere unnoticed. Embroider in white silk on violet satin and carry with you. It may also be engraved on a ring or an amulet.

Note: *the snake chasing its tail represents the Voodoo loa Damballah, a powerful force for good. He is known as the "serpent god," and will help the wearer to avoid making mistakes, to make right decisions, and to overcome all problems. This talisman is especially valuable to those who already have a strong degree of natural intuition, and others who are interested in developing strong perception. The three wavy lines attached to a black ball merely concentrate and direct the forces of Damballah. An offering of boiled eggs and flour must be given to this loa in order to make him take action. His favorite day is Thursday.*

TO HAVE PROPHETIC DREAMS OF THE FUTURE

Sandalwood Incense	**1/2 cup**
Myrrh Incense	**2 teaspoons**
Orris Root (crushed)	**1/2 cup**
Frankincense Resin	**3 teaspoons**
Irish Moss	**1/2 cup**
Spikenard (crushed)	**2 teaspoons**

Blend all of the above ingredients (see appendix for sources) in a small bowl, cover tightly, and hide in a dark corner until needed.One teaspoonful is to be burned every evening just as you prepare for bed. Burn it only on a piece of ***Fast Lighting Charcoal.*** Also put a little of the same mixture in a ***red flannel bag*** with a ***Black Cat's Bone.*** Sew the bag tightly together and place it under your pillow.

Following these instructions, according to Anatol Pierre, is said to make you have visions in your sleep. You will dream prophetically and then be able to correctly interpret these dreams. In so doing, you will then know what steps to take to best influence your fate.

Anatol Pierre was a Catholic middle-aged octoroon who claimed a distant kinship to Marie Laveau, as did so many other Voodooists. He was a highly emotional, sharp-tongued Voodoo Priest in New Orleans of the 1930's. Pierre was a specialist in many areas of Voodoo and he placed what he called "guaranteed death hexes," as well as potent love charms. He built an elaborate "temple" in his house where all rituals were conducted. And he was able to attract a huge following almost overnight, in part because of the effectiveness of his spells, and in part because of his personal magnetism.

18

To Increase Fertility

TO MAKE YOU MORE POTENT

This fabulous talisman makes a man or a woman more fertile. It causes pregnancy in couples who are childless and it makes a man's penis more rigid when making love. But this talisman must be taken off and placed under the mattress when having sex in order to be effective.

Embroider in ***bright red on white satin*** and carry with you. It may also be engraved on a ring or an amulet. ***Note:*** The crossed penis in the above talisman represents the Voodoo loa *Marinette*, a powerful spirit of fertility and sexuality. The other symbols are simply made to contain and direct her forces as necessary. If thistalisman is used for any other purpose than is outlined above, *Marinette* is said to become very malicious, a constant troublemaker, and an antagonized. She demands an offering of semen rubbed in chicken feathers before unleashing her powerful spirit forces for the good of her subjects. She looks with great favor upon those who have oral sex as a prelude to intercourse. Marinette's special day is Wednesday and a sexual interlude on this day is believed to bring immediate results.

TO RAISE A MAN'S SPERM COUNT

Aloes Powder	**1 teaspoon**
Musk Powder	**1 teaspoon**
Parchment Paper	**1 piece**
Genital Hairs	**3**
Witch's Oil	**1 bottle**

According to High Priestess Malvina Latour, you should blend the first 2 ingredients just before going to bed. Put this mixture on a piece of burning ***Fast Lighting Charcoal*** in an incense burner or on a plain white saucer. As the incense smolders, take the parchment paper and write on it the name of the man who needs help. Use only ***Dove's Blood Ink*** for this purpose or the spell will not be effective. Allow the ink to completely dry and then lay 3 of his genital hairs on it. As each hair is placed over his name, repeat aloud the following invocation:

Diana, Diana, Diana
O most powerful Diana
Raise the power of this unfortunate man
Allow him to impregnate his loved one
By all your love Diana
Increase his manliness
Diana, Diana, Diana
Help him to easily father children

Then sprinkle the hairs with 9 drops of ***Witch's Oil*** and quickly burn the parchment and hairs until they turn to ashes. Collect the ashes and blend them with the ashes from the burned incense mixture. Scatter these ashes under the bed of the man who needs assistance. Or if you're casting this spell for someone else, and you do not have access to the bedroom of the husband, simply scatter the ashes towards the four points of the compass. As you do this, speak the following words:

O great gods of wind, help me
Carry these ashes to where he lies
May no time be wasted
Goddess Diana, bless him
He is now aided, he can make children
The deed is done, the deed is done

The above ritualistic charm was often utilized by High Priestess Malvina Latour as a means of giving a man new virility. She ruled New Orlean's Voodoo from 1869 to 1890 and was described by George W. Cable in the April, 1881, issue of *Century Magazine*, as being: "a bright mulattress of about forty-eight, of extremely handsome figure, dignified bearing, and a face indicative of a comparatively high order of intelligence."

TO INCREASE CHANCES OF BECOMING PREGNANT

Basil Leaves are considered to be a sacred herb in ancient Voodoo lore. Properly prepared, this herb is said by Don Pedro to make women fertile who had previously been unable to conceive. It is held in high esteem in all Voodoo cults today.

The use of ***Basil Leaves***is quite a simple undertaking according to Pedro. Just put 1 tablespoon in 2 quarts of hot water. Let it soak in a sunny corner of the house for 7 full days before using. Then sprinkle a little of this mixture all around the bed in which lovemaking is to take place. Rub some of it lightly over the penis of your mate before intercourse is begun. This should be initiated while his penis is still soft and pliable and continued until it becomes erect and fully extended. Be sure to cover the entire length of the shaft and especially under the foreskin.

Or, better yet, gargle with some of the warm liquid and after spitting it out, lightly flit over your husband's penis with your extended tongue's tip. If his penis is not yet hard, take the very end of its head between your pursed lips and draw its full length into your mouth with strong suction. Then pretend it is a piece of candy and imagine you are trying to make it dissolve in your mouth. Run and lick all around the shaft with your tongue as you apply even more firm suction with an up and down movement of your head. Hold fast to his penis with your lips until it becomes erect and throbbing. You may then proceed with sexual intercourse in the usual way until a climax is reached by both partners.

To further aid in becoming pregnant, season all your meals with ***Basil.*** Both the husband and the wife should eat together by candle light, and then make love as directed above, in the light of a flickering *Red Jumbo Candle.*

The above ritual was long recommended by the notorious Don Pedro, a powerful Voodoo King in New Orleans during the 1850 to 1890 period. Pedro was a highly regarded love and sex specialist in Voodoo circles of the time. One of his fertility rites was raided in 1855 by Captain Eugene Mazart of the New Orleans Police Department. The men in blue caught 12 beautiful white women and 12 handsome black men, all nude, performing a lewd Voodoo dance. Sexual relations of various kinds were obviously being enjoyed by a number of the participants. Don Pedro was in the center of the orgiastic group conducting the ritual as well as sampling the wares of the various damsels. All were arrested and fined a small amount before being released.

19

To Bring Financial Gain

TO GAIN FINANCIALLY

High John the Conqueror Root	**3 pieces**
High John the Conqueror Candle	**1**

Reverend Father Joe Watson said to take 1 piece of ***High John the Conqueror Root*** and wrap a dollar bill securely around it. Fasten with a rubber band or piece of string so it won't come off. Put this in your purse or a pocket and carry with you at all times, or tie a white cotton string around it and wear it as an amulet around the neck. In either case, never leave the house without this money attracting charm.

Secondly, burn a ***High John the Conqueror Candle*** each day to help in your endeavor. This will make the universal vibrations more favorable to your financial needs. As the candle flickers, concentrate on money, and roll another piece of ***High John the Conqueror Root*** around in your hands.

As an added aid to obtaining money, take a third piece of this same root and boil it in a quart of ***fresh rain water.*** After it has cooled, sprinkle a little of this liquid around the house and rub some on your hands and forehead.

Each of the above three methods is said to have been successful for a great number of people in time of financial need. Any of the above is usually powerful enough to achieve the desired end result, but most Voodooists recommend undertaking all 3 to guarantee a favorable response from the good vibratory forces.

TO GET MORE MONEY

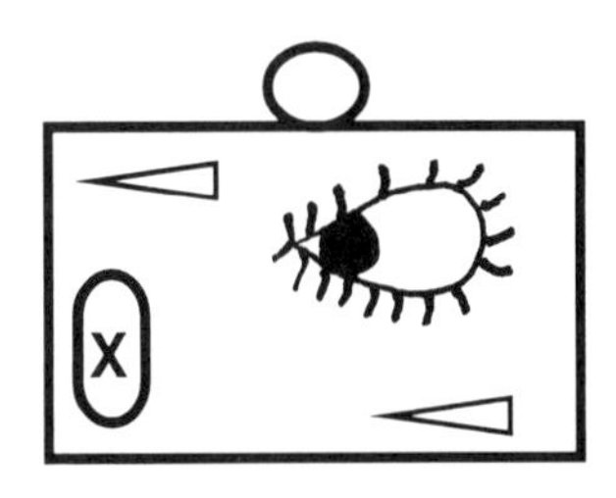

This talisman is said to attract great wealth to anyone who owns and wears it faithfully. It is an excellent aid for increasing business, for winning money in contests, and to help obtain an increase in pay from your boss. Money will often come from unexpected sources. Embroider in **light green silk on dark green satin** and carry with you. It may also be engraved on a ring or an amulet. ***Note:*** The crossed eye in the above talisman represents the Voodoo loa *Onzoncaire*, a special spirit force with a hunger for money. The other symbols are simply made to contain and direct the power of this loa. Anything having to do with money can be accomplished by *Onzoncaire*. An offering of a quart of whiskey is required before this loa will consent to taking any action.

TO INDUCE OTHERS TO GIVE YOU MONEY

Jumbo Green Candle	**1**
Money Oil	**1 bottle**
Jezebel Root	**1 piece**

Take the ***Jumbo Green Candle*** and rub it down carefully with a little ***Money Oil.*** Then place it on a plain white saucer and light. Let the candle melt down completely, and then force the ***Jezebel Root*** into the middle of the soft wax. Roll this up into a ball and set in a cool place until it hardens.

When the wax ball is hard, immediately go out to a cemetery and bury it near a headstone. Or better still, find a freshly duggrave and drop it in. Kick a little dirt over the ball so it will not be seen. Then repeat the following invocation, 3 times:

O Jezebel, O Jezebel
Let someone give me money!
O Jezebel, O Jezebel
Bring me lots of cash!

The above must be repeated aloud as you stand directly over the spot where the wax ball was buried. You must be certain no one is close at hand to see or hear you do this or the spell will be broken. Then turn away and quickly return home. Do not look back under any circumstances!

This money charm was one of the great Doctor John's favorites. He was an expert in making money himself and was able to amass a large fortune while a Voodoo King in New Orleans. Instead of using a saucer as directed above, Doctor John used human skulls as candle holders. These skulls were stolen from graveyards throughout the city. This black man was still tall and handsome in his later years, and he wore a neat white beard. He loved frilly white shirts, expensively tailored clothing and imported shoes. John owned many slaves. He left his mark on American Voodoo for he was the first High Priest to blend Catholicism with snake worship. He ran a tight Voodoo organization and had agents throughout New Orleans working for him.

TO FIND SOME CASH

This is Doctor Jenkins' special formula for making powerful amulets designed for helping find money. The amulet must be worn around your neck on a chain or string, or at least carried with you always in a purse or pocket. You will need the following ingredients:

Frankincense	**1 teaspoon**
Cloves Powder	**2/3 teaspoon**
Bay	**2/3 teaspoon**
Angelica	**2/3 teaspoon**
Cinnamon Powder	**1/2 teaspoon**
Saltpeter	**A pinch**
Money Powder	**A pinch**

Blend all of the above ingredients thoroughly and quickly put them into a ***red flannel sack.*** Sew the top tightly shut and then sprinkle it with 9 drops of ***Money Oil.*** Never leave your house without this flannel bag.

To further aid you in finding money, blend the same amount of the above mixture and place it on a plain white saucer. Burn half each morning upon arising, and half each night before going to bed. This is said to create favorable money vibrations throughout your place of residence.

Doctor Samuel Jenkins was a darkly handsome black man in his forties when he became famous for his Voodoo conjuring. He operated around Marrero, Louisiana during the 1930's and specialized in card readings. Jenkins claimed to be a clairvoyant and said he was the greatest psychic ever to live. He did have a huge following, mostly white upper class clients, who swore by his numerous uncanny predictions.

20

To Overcome Hatred

TO STOP SOMEONE FROM HATING YOU

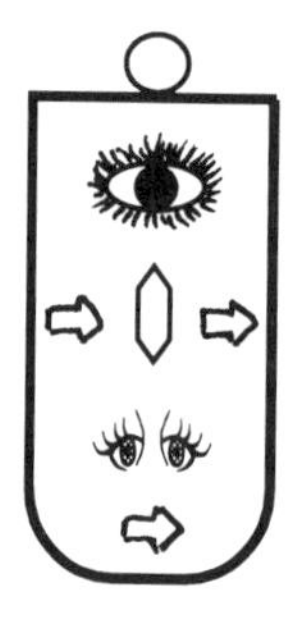

This fantastic talisman forces a former loved one or a good friend to cease despising its possessor. The spirit forces associated with the talisman also help to overcome your own feelings of hatred. It offers protection from any enemies who may be planning physical harm, or who intend to create great anguish in some other way.

Embroider in ***orange silk on violet satin*** and carry with you. It may also be engraved on a ring or an amulet. ***Note:*** The three eyes in the above talisman represent the Voodoo loa *Ogoun Bedagaris*, whose power is surpassed only by the loa *Damballah, Erzalie* and *Agarou Tonnerre.* The other symbols are simply made to contain and direct the powers of this loa. *Ogoun Bedagaris* requires offerings of fresh, still warm rooster blood before he will consent to taking any action in your behalf. Some of this blood must be consumed by the talisman's owner.

TO REMOVE YOUR OWN FEELINGS OF HATRED

An old adage in Voodoo worship, and one often repeated by Doctor Moses, is "one cannot love when full of hate and one cannot hate who is full of love." Therefore, Moses' method of replacing hatred with love and understanding has always been popular among Voodooists. You will need the following ingredients:

Powdered Mace	**1 teaspoon**
Lovage	**1 teaspoon**
Jasmine	**2 teaspoons**
Tonka Beans (powdered)	**1 teaspoon**
Juniper Berries (crushed)	**1 teaspoon**

Blend all of these materials in a wooden bowl, and when thoroughly mixed, put them into a small white cotton sack. Tie the top tightly together and then draw some hot bath water. Drop the bag into the bath water and leave it to soak until the water becomes cool enough for bathing.

Then remove the bag, wring it out, and place in a pint jar. Cap the jar tightly and save the bag to use over and over. Then take a leisurely bath. This special bathing charm is said to make you more magnetic, friendly, and attractive to others, especially those people you formerly couldn't get along with very well.

This concoction was developed by Doctor Freddie Moses, a popular South Rampart Street conjure man of the 1940's. This black Voodoo practitioner was said to be powerful with his magic, and he was able to attract a large following. He too was a man who had a long string of black and white lovers, and was considered to be quite a lady's man. Moses followed Rockford Lewis into the mail-order Voodoo business because of its popularity on a national scale.

TO STOP HATE FROM HURTING YOU

This is a wonderful charm according to Mama Levasseur, for overcoming hatred and to prevent it from harming you. To make it properly you will need the following ingredients:

Patchouly	**1 teaspoon**
Bayberry Powder	**1/2 teaspoon**
Cloves Powder	**1/2 teaspoon**
Linden Flowers(crushed)	**1/4 cup**
Basil (crushed)	**1 teaspoon**
Saltpeter	**1/4 teaspoon**
Tonka Beans (crushed)	**1/4 cup**
Jasmine	**1/2 cup**

Blend all of the above materials in a wooden bowl, cover, and set aside in a cool place until needed. Then burn a small amount of it each evening at sunset and each morning upon arising. Burn this only on a piece of ***Fast Lighting Charcoal.***

Put 2 teaspoons of the mixture in a ***red flannel bag or a small chamois sack*** and sew the top tightly together. Carry this with you at all times when away from home. Or you may instead wish to wear the bag on a string or chain around the neck. Either way will suffice.

Angele Levasseur operated as a Voodoo High Priestess in New Orleans during the late 1800's. She was a horrible old crone who tried to imitate Marie Laveau for a number of years after Laveau's forced retirement in 1869. This Voodoo Queen was almost drowned on Lake Pontchartrain in 1894 when a terrible storm came up during one of her ceremonies.

TO CHANGE HATRED TO LOVE

When you want to change feelings of hatred to those of love and sexual desire in someone of the opposite sex, conjure Doctor Ed Murphy suggested the use of ***Dill Seed*** to do the job quickly. He claimed marvelous results can be obtained if a few simple steps are properly carried out.

The first step is to add seven grains of ***Dill Seed*** to a tub of boiling hot bath water. Let the seeds soak until the water becomes just warm enough to comfortably bathe in. Anyone who takes such a bath is said to be made physically irresistible to a person of the opposite sex. The effect of the seed-bath beguiles them when in your presence and it will induce the person to forget all previous harsh feelings.

If this doesn't seem to do the trick, then follow it up by serving some wine to your reluctant guest, but before doing so, prepare the wine with this special formula. Add a few ***Dill Seeds*** to a saucepan of hot wine. Let it simmer together for a period of 7 minutes. Then set aside to cool. When the wine is cold, strain into a bottle and cork tightly until ready to use. Serve this to the person who despises you and they immediately begin to change. Be careful with this mixture for it is said to also have the capability of arousing the most animal passion in people of the opposite sex.

Conjure Doctor Murphy was a very old, black man who practiced Voodoo in Mississippi of the 1920's. He was believed to wield awesome power and he was highly respected by people in the area. Doctor Ed spent most of his time in meditation and was seldom ever seen outside his shanty. But whenever he did go out for anything, he was never without his crooked wooden cane. Murphy was best known as a specialist in the use of herbs, plants, roots and leaves. In fact, people in the Mississippi delta called him the "Root Doctor."

21

To Make Right Decisions

TO MAKE CORRECT DECISIONS WHILE UNDER STRESS

Peace Oil	**1 bottle**
John the Conqueror Incense	**1 packet**
Helping Hand Incense	**1 packet**
White Candle of Peace	**1**

Each morning, upon arising, you must willingly take a bath. Put 3 drops of ***Peace Oil*** in your hot bath water and then let it cool until it is right for bathing. Then, after completely and thoroughly drying off, anoint your forehead with a little of this same oil.

Now burn a little ***John the Conqueror Incense*** the first day and some ***Helping Hand Incense*** the next day. Continue burning these two incenses on alternate days, but never miss a day or the spell will not be effective.

Lastly, take a piece of ***parchment paper*** and write on it 9 times, with ***Dove's Blood Ink,*** the word **"PEACE."** Place this on a clean white saucer under the ***White Candle* of *Peace.*** Light the candle and allow it to burn until you leave the house for the day. Meanwhile, after lighting the candle, read aloud ***Psalm 137.***

Follow these instructions carefully, on a daily basis and you will find understanding, mental harmony and peace of mind where confusion presently reigns. Try to be more cheerful when under stress and smile rather than frown when hard decisions must be made while under extreme pressure. This Voodoo charm was used by a great number of business people in Charleston, South Carolina and in New Orleans, Louisiana, during the dawning period of the nineteenth century. It is still popular today in those areas of the United States as well as in all other sections where Voodoo is prevalent. Marie Laveau was one of the charm's chief advocates in New Orleans during her terrifying reign over all Voodoo cults in the 1800's.

TO HELP YOU DECIDE ON ANYTHING

This powerful talisman is said to be wonderful whenever important decisions must be made. It helps clear the mind while the wearer is under any type pressure from outside himself. All uncertainty will be quickly overcome and a new feeling of self-confidence will prevail. Embroider in ***dark blue silk and gray satin*** and carry with you. It may also be engraved on a ring or an amulet. ***Note:*** The square-headed man in the above talisman represents the Voodoo loa *Zacamica,* who protects the interests of hesitant people. He especially loves those who are poor and downtrodden. The other symbols are simply made to help intensify and guide the spirit forces of *Zacamica* when he is called upon for aid. This loa enjoys an offering of buttered slices of toast before going into action on your behalf. And he always prefers that the toast be made from homemade bread.

TO USE IN ALL IMPORTANT DECISIONS

Take a ***Magnetic Lodestone*** and anoint it well with equal amounts of ***Magnet Oil*** and ***John the Conqueror Oil.*** Wrap the lodestone in *a* ***Seal of Spiritual Assistance*** and tie with a piece of ***red cotton yarn or red ribbon.***

This talisman must be worn or carried with you at all times in order to be fully effective. It is said to be extremely good for helping make correct decisions, concerning business and other personal problems, and even attracting good luck when it is most needed. And it should never be shown or loaned to anyone else under any circumstances.

This talisman was developed by Miss Jackson, a powerful Voodoo Queen in New Orleans of the 1850's. She is said to have used it as well, as she did numerous other charms which called for lodestone as an important part of the ingredients. She and Octave Labeau were both lesser Queens under the iron rule of High Priestess Marie Laveau. They and a violent High Priest called Leon Janpier (Marie's lover) all worked for Laveau and each had a huge following of their own.

WHEN YOU MUST DECIDE QUICKLY

According to Queen Lala, this talisman is good for anyone who has a job with responsibility. It should be used when decisions must be made on the spot. Make this wonderful charm only on the first Sunday of a new moon.

Take a clean piece of ***parchment paper,*** and in ***Dove's Blood Ink,*** write the following words:

Non licet ponare in egarbona quia pretium sanguinis.

Lay a ***Magnetic Lodestone*** on the paper and fold each corner toward the center until the writing cannot possibly be seen by any other eyes. Tie the parchment with a piece of ***yellow yarn, ribbon, or even string.*** Carry it in a pocket, purse, or on a gold chain around the neck. No one must be allowed to know you wear this talisman or its effectiveness will be totally negated.

Mama Lala, Queen Lala, or simply Lala, was a Voodoo High Priestess in New Orleans during the 1940's. She first gained a terrifying reputation for her outstanding success with black magic and evil spell casting. Miss Lala claimed to have later reformed. She then became a specialist in unhexing, love amulets and making only good charms. Mama Lala's power was once so feared that people crossed the street in order to avoid passing close to her. The look of evil in her eyes made many associates cringe upon meeting her face to face.

TO OVERCOME INDECISIVENESS

According to all powerful Voodoo Kings and Queens throughout the United States today, the ***Wild Yam*** is still one of the best items to use when a person is wishy washy. Just put some ***Wild Yam*** (about 1 tablespoon) in a quart of boiling water. Cover the jar or kettle and set it aside to cool. Then hide the liquid in a dark corner and leave it to soak well for 7 full days. Rinse your hands with a little of this mixture before going to work and all indecisiveness will quickly be overcome.

Some Voodoo practitioners still use this type ***Wild Yam*** rinse on their hands just before entering into any sort of a healing ritual. It is believed to possess-powerful spiritual qualities which aid in bringing better health to those who suffer with many kinds of crippling illnesses. Voodoo High Priestesses in New York, Chicago, Los Angeles, New Orleans and Charleston cite numerous instances where successful healing was accomplished by "laying of hands" after rinsing with this mixture.

Mama Etoine, a 97 year old Voodoo faith healer, claims to have been extremely successful with her medical cures. She professes to have helped mostly the poor people in her area of the nation. But many of her regular customers are those who belong to the higher social strata. Mama mumbles out the names of show business personalities, business people and even important politicians who have sought her assistance.

22

To Avoid Accidents

TO AVERT AN ACCIDENT

This potent talisman will protect the wearer from all accidents both while traveling and while in the home. It is one of the best protective devices known in Voodoo practice today. The talisman will also spread its protective vibrations over loved ones. Embroider in ***pink silk on dark brown satin*** and carry with you. It may also be engraved on a ring or an amulet. ***Note:*** The boat in the above talisman represents the Voodoo loa *Agwe.* Annual Voodoo rites are held to honor and appease this spirit force. The other symbols are simply made to help concentrate and direct his power in behalf of the talisman's owner. *Agwe* demands an offering of a cooked red rooster before he will take appropriate steps to watch over you and your loved ones and to take action in your behalf. Brown candles should be burned after sundown on the third Wednesday of each month in order to keep *Agwe* happy.

JULIA JACKSON'S METHOD OF STOPPING ACCIDENTAL PREGNANCY

This wonderful charm is to be used by women before partaking of any sexual relations. It is said to prevent pregnancy if faithfully undertaken. You will need the following ingredients:

Attraction Powder	**1 packet**
Magnet Oil	**1 bottle**
Lucky Nine Mixture	**1 bottle**
Maiden Hairs	**3**
Seal of Orion	**1**

First you must take a warm bath each morning upon arising after a sexual interlude. Then carefully powder yourself down lightly with ***Attraction Powder.*** Rub a little ***Magnet Oil*** and ***Lucky Nine Mixture*** on your forehead and both upper thighs near the vagina. Then carefully clip 3 longer hairs from the genital region and wear them near your heart, in a bra if you use one. Read aloud ***Psalm 65.***

Take the ***Seal of Orion*** and put it in a ***small chamois sack or a red flannel bag.*** Carry this with you at all times, except of course when making love. It should then be worn around your neck during intercourse in order to be effective, unless of course, you have an oral fetish, and this is the manner which you make your partner reach his climax. In such cases, the protection of the ***Seal of Orion*** is not needed.

Julia Jackson reminds us that a certain amount of sacrifice is necessary in all Voodoo rituals. Protection from pregnancy is guaranteed, according to her, in your journey through life if the above instructions are faithfully carried out to completion. Miss Jackson, or Queen Julia, was a highly respected Voodoo High Priestess during the 1940's. She was a dark black, intelligent, over 6 feet tall, and had slightly crossed eyes. This woman was sometimes called "Queen of Perdido Street," which is about 2 blocks above Canal Street in New Orleans. Julia completely dominated the section just off South Rampart Street, known as "Lakeside," a low income black section of the city.

TO PREVENT ACCIDENTS FROM HAPPENING

This very old Voodoo charm was found written down in a yellowed ledger book. It was hidden in the attic of an old and empty Charleston, South Carolina home, back before the Civil War. Here is what you will need:

Seal of Mephistophilis	**1**
High Conquering Oil	**1 bottle**
Uncrossing Bath	**1 bottle**
Confusion Powder	**1 packet**
Get Away Powder	**1 packet**

First anoint the ***Seal of Mephistophilis*** with 7 drops of ***High Conquering Oil*** and carry it with you in a purse or pocket at all times. This seal must be anointed every 3 days without fail or the consequences of a serious accident may befall you. Also sprinkle a little of this same oil on your ear lobes, wrists and thighs.

One teaspoon of ***Uncrossing Bath*** is to be put in your daily bath water as added protection from accidents. After finishing bathing, dry off, dress quickly, and run outside. Walk all around the house and by each door and window, sprinkle equal amounts of ***Confusion Powder*** and ***Get Away Powder.*** This is said to confound the evil forces which may force you into situations where accidents could harm you.

The above procedure is highly recommended in the old ledger. It is said to be especially good for people who seem to be accident prone, and those who seem to be unfortunate as a way of life. Besides doing all of the above, you should make a daily practice of reading ***Psalm 52*** upon arising.

MADAME CAZAUNOUX'S WAY OF HALTING ACCIDENTAL DEATH

The proper use of *Helping Hand Incense* in the home is an old requirement in Voodoo practice when serious accidents are to be prevented. This special protective incense must be faithfully burned each evening during the following hours:

Sunday	**7:00 pm**
Monday	**10:00 pm**
Tuesday	**11:00 pm**
Wednesday	**8:00 pm**
Thursday	**5:00 pm**
Friday	**9:00 pm**
Saturday	**6:00 pm**

It is always best to burn the incense on a piece of ***Fast Lighting Charcoal.*** After the ***Helping Hand Incense*** begins to smolder, light a ***Gold Candle.*** Then repeat the following invocation, 3 times, and extinguish the candle.

Accidental death will be thwarted
(Your name) will not face this dire problem
It draws away from me and my home
It swings away from me and my home
It is my destiny to survive all accidents
Accidental death is not possible now!

The above ritualistic charm was used by a little known, but extremely powerful Voodoo Queen who practiced under the name of Madame Cazaunoux. This old quadroon was a small, wrinkled and stooped lady of about 80 years. Her real name was Agatha May Wilson and she quite popular during the early 1900's. Cazaunoux had a rather large following in her day but she was quickly forgotten after she died.

23

To Cast Evil Spells

BEUREGARD'S WAY OF PLACING HEXES

Take a small piece of ***parchment paper*** and write down the name of your enemy in ***Dove's Blood Ink.*** Do this backwards, 9 times, and immediately light a ***Black Double Action Reverse Candle.*** Allow the candle to completely burn itself out, but as it flickers, blend the following ingredients:

Double Cross Powder	**1/4 teaspoon**
Graveyard Dust	**3 teaspoons**
Skunk Cabbage Root	**1 piece**
Vetivert Powder	**1 teaspoon**
War Water	**3 tablespoons**

Now mix all of the above with some of the candle drippings and set aside in a dark place until needed. Burn the parchment paper with the names written on it. Collect the ashes and mix them with a little of the soft melted candle wax. Form into a small ball and place this in a bottle of ***Four Thieves Vinegar.*** Use this liquid, after the sun goes down, to sprinkle your enemy's door and front yard. Return home and go to bed.

Wait 3 full days and then return to your enemy's house. This time take the mixture previously set aside and carefully sprinkle it all around his front door. Be sure to get some of it on the door itself. Quickly return home and sprinkle some ***Dragon's Blood Powder*** around your own doors. Burn a little ***Spiritual Attraction Incense*** in your home and you will be safe from revenge. These items will protect you from any evil forces unleashed against your enemy, and from spells he or she may try to place against you in return.

This old charm was created by one of 1860 New Orleans' famed High Priests of Voodoo. He called himself Doctor Beuregard, and he was a contemporary of Doctor Jacks, the man who was without doubt the leading love specialist in his day. Beuregard was an unkempt, aged black man who originally came from the hills of Kentucky. His hair reached down past his waist when it was combed out. But his hair was usually worn rolled and knotted. This man was fearful looking to say the least, he scared people as he passed them on the street.

POWER TO DESTROY

This unique talisman is said to contain the power of destroying everyone and everything in its possessor's path. It is said to be able to cause earthquakes, floods, hail, lightning, etc. Embroider in ***silver silk on poppy-red satin*** and carry with you. It may also be engraved on a ring or an amulet.

Note: The winged female in the above talisman represents the Voodoo loa *Ezili-Couer-Noir,* one of the most black-hearted of all spirit forces. She is totally evil and extremely dangerous. This particular talisman should be worn only while casting evil spells, *and this must be accomplished only at midnight on a moonless night. Keep the talisman carefully wrapped in black cotton and hide it in a dark corner of a closed closet at all other times. The other symbols are designed to restrain the evil forces of* Ezili-Couer-Noir *when a spell is not being cast. And these symbols protect the wearer of the talisman from all harm. This terrible loa requires an offering of 1 cup of warm black rooster blood before she will take action on your behalf.*

JOSEPH MELON'S METHOD OF CROSSING ENEMIES

This old curse is said to be especially good when you are being pushed around and pressured by someone who wishes to harm you. Wait until your patience runs out and then start creating this special hexing charm. It is said to disarm the person causing the trouble and will bring hatred and violence raining down upon their head. You will need the following ingredients:

Four Thieves Vinegar	**1 small bottle**
Black Arts Oil	**1 bottle**
Black Candle	**1**

Pour the ***Four Thieves Vinegar*** *into a shallow dish and dip a piece of* ***parchment*** *in it. When the paper is soaked, take it out and set aside to dry. Then take some* ***Dove's Blood Ink*** *and write the name of your enemy. Rub the* ***Black Candle*** *with 13 drops of* ***Black Arts Oil*** *and light it. Hold the parchment paper over the flame, and as it burns, murmur the following invocation:*

> ***Here stands (name), mine enemy, all alone! You are friendless! Frustration shall overtake you! You shall be rendered defenseless! All your plans are voided! Fear, doubt, worry and hesitation surround you! Discord and fury creep into your horrid life! You are doomed to dearly pay for tormenting me! You are doomed - doomed - doomed!***

The above method of placing a curse is attributed to a Voodoo King called Joseph Melon, a black man who flourished in the 1840's and 1850's. He claimed to be a witch doctor and publicly danced in Congo Square during hexing rituals. Melon was feared by young and old alike, was considered to be the meanest man alive, and was violently vicious. He was a moose of a man who always carried a book and walked with a cane. Joseph Melon was almost totally evil and primarily practiced black magic, specializing in curses and creating terrible spells.

A POWERFUL HEXING CHARM

If you have an enemy and wish to curse him, this old Voodoo charm of Hoodoo Mag's will accomplish the purpose. It must be initiated at midnight. Blend the following ingredients:

Black Arts Incense	**1 teaspoon**
Chicory Powder	**1 tablespoon**
Crossing Incense	**1/4 cup**

Put a little of this mixture on a saucer and light. Then immediately light a ***Black Hexing Candle.*** Repeat the name of your enemy 7 times, pause, then 9 more,times. Let the incense burn itself out and then extinguish the candle. Do this every night, for 9 successive nights, and the curse will take effect. To further insure results, collect the incense ashes from the entire 9 nights of burning and sprinkle these in the yard of your enemy's house.

The New Orleans *Daily Crescent* best describes this 1850 period Voodoo Queen as: "a black hellcat named Margaret, a slave . . . and known to black people throughout the city as Hoodoo Nag, the queen or high priestess of the mystic order of the Voudous.... The priestess claims to have the exclusive business of compounding and retailing bags containing charms and bottles containing direct curses.

24

To Change Your Personality

TO IMPROVE YOUR PERSONALITY

This unique talisman gives its possessor the ability to change his or her personal characteristics at will. It is said to be an excellent means of self-improvement for these having unusual personality quirks or some weakness of character. Embroider in ***yellow silk on orange satin*** and carry with you. It may also be engraved on a ring or an amulet. ***Note:*** The cross struck by a lightning bolt represents the Voodoo loa *Achille-Piquant* who is best known for his good deeds. This spirit speaks through his nose and has great sympathy for anyone desiring to become a better person. The other symbols are simply made to intensify and direct his powerful forces when called upon. *Achille-Piquant* requires an offering of raw fish sprinkled with a little pepper before he will take any positive action in a believer's behalf. The wearer of the talisman must willingly eat some of this fish, as it is being prepared for *Achille-Piquant.*

TO OVERCOME PERSONALITY QUIRKS

This very old Voodoo charm was still being used in the 1930's and 1940's by a conjure woman called Mrs. Crobuzon. It was originally devised as an aid in overcoming specific personality traits. And it is said to bring success in developing a stronger will power as well as guaranteeing success in formulating a better, more appealing personality. You will need the following ingredients:

Frankincense	**1/3 cup**
Myrrh Incense	**1/4 cup**
Sandalwood Incense	**1/4 cup**
Sacred Bark (crushed)	**1/2 cup**
Saltpeter	**1/2 teaspoon**
Mandrake Root (crushed)	**1 teaspoon**
Saffron Powder	**2 teaspoons**

Blend all of the above materials in a wooden bowl, cover tightly, and set in a cool dark place until needed. Then, starting on a Sunday night at sundown, place a little of this mixture on a piece of burning ***Charcoal.*** As it smolders, anoint a ***Seven Day Trinity Candle*** with ***Success Oil.*** Light the candle and recite aloud ***Psalm 4.*** Allow the candle to continue burning until you go to bed that night.

Follow these specific instructions daily until your goal has been accomplished. It works quickly for some people, but takes longer to be effective for others. Do not be discouraged if results are not immediate.

Mrs. Crobuzon was a poor old homeless black crone who many people claimed was a witch. She was one of the most horrifying Voodoo practitioners ever known in New Orleans and was said by Julia Jackson to have "sold her soul to the devil." Crobuzon was accused of having murdered 1 of her children each year as a sacrifice to Satan. She had already killed 12 of them when High Priestess Jackson knew her.

ANNIE GOULD'S WAY OF OPENING YOUR MIND

Quince Seed	**1/2 teaspoon**
Queen of the Meadow	**1/2 teaspoon**
Lucky Blueing Water	**1 bottle**

Put the ***Quince Seed*** and the ***Queen of the Meadow*** in the ***Lucky Blueing Water,*** cover tightly, and set aside for 7 days to soak in a cool, dark place. Strain the mixture through muslin and add a few drops to the water in which you wash your clothing. This wonderful old charm is said to expand the mind of anyone who wears clothing so treated. They will become interested in many more things and as a result will be happier, more popular, in demand, and respected by others.

This charm came into popularity during the 1870's when it was successfully utilized by a powerful woman named Annie Gould. She teamed up with Doctor James Alexander and Doctor Sol (Solomon Hastings) to challenge the authority of Voodoo High Priestess Malvina Latour. Annie's approach to Voodoo was primarily selling charms and amulets through the mail. Her home on Monroe Street in New Orleans was raided by the police in 1894. Numerous skulls, humans and dogs, were found as were jars of dried snakes, toads, lizards, etc.

DOCTOR DUKE'S WAY TO BRING POPULARITY

Marigold Powder	**1 teaspoon**
Lemon Verbena Powder	**1 teaspoon**
Mace Powder	**1 teaspoon**
CalamusPowder	**1 teaspoon**
Hops Powder	**1 teaspoon**
Magnolia Herb (crushed)	**1 teaspoon**
Quince Seed (crushed)	**1 teaspoon**

Blend all of the above ingredients and put them into 1 gallon of boiling water. Cover the kettle, remove from the stove, and set aside to cool. Then put the mixture into a large crock or jug and set it in a cool, dark place for 9 days to soak. Strain the mixture on the morning of the tenth day. Use 1/4 cup in your daily bath water and others will immediately begin to show more respect and admiration for you. Your popularity with members of both sexes will climb to undreamed of heights.

This charm is credited to Doctor Duke who operated in New Orleans around 1930. Duke was over 50 years old and developed a great reputation for his work in herbal conjuring. He claimed to be an expert in many areas of Voodoo, but said he was best at unhexing people. Duke claimed to have the power of driving evil spirits out of and away from anyone.

TO BECOME MORE RELIABLE

In early Louisiana Territory Voodoo practice, the ***Rhubarb Root*** was often used in both cooking and as an amulet. A little of this root was crushed and added to the foods being prepared for the dinner table. A string was often attached to a small piece of the root and it was worn around the neck of any person trying to overcome a weakness of character.

Rhubarb Root is believed to have the uncanny power of making a man or woman more reliable and trustworthy. Many great Voodoo Queens and Kings recommended this treatment for men who couldn't seem to remain faithful. It was also deemed excellent for married women who found it difficult to reject the amorous advances of male friends.

25

To Ward Off Evil Spirits

TO KEEP EVIL SPIRITS AWAY FROM YOUR HOUSE

Angelica Powder was one of Marie Laveau's most popular recommendations for stopping the machinations of evil forces. It is said to ward off all forms of evil and it is quite simple to use. To protect your home, just sprinkle all 4 corners in each room with a little of this potent powder. No bad spirits will dare enter and try to create havoc in the lives of those who reside within.

To gain protection for yourself when outside the home, carry a small ***red flannel sack*** of ***Angelica Powder*** with you at all times. Do not lose this or the wrath of many evil forces are said to rain down upon your head.

This very old protective charm was devised by the most notorious Queen of New Orleans' Voodoo in the early 1800's. She swore by its effectiveness and was to claim many successes with persons who paid dearly for one of her famous protective "conjure bags."

One youthful prostitute, a regular customer of Laveau's, was saved, or so she believed, by the power of this lady's unusual protective charm. She had been violently attacked while on her way home after a long hard night's work. Just before her assailant was able to plunge his dagger between her bared, upturned breasts, he spotted the red flannel bag hanging there limply between them. Instead of completing his dastardly deed, the obviously terrified man dropped his long knife on the spot and turned to run. He went but three short steps before dropping dead in his tracks. His death was attributed without question to the power of the famous ***Angelica Powder*** spell. Who could possibly convince the thankful prostitute otherwise?

TO PREVENT THE HARM OF ALL EVIL SPIRITS

This talisman is extremely powerful when used to stop evil spirit forces from inflicting their wrath on you. It helps to overcome harmful black magic spells. An enemy who tries to place a curse on the possessor will be stopped in his or her tracks. Embroider in ***gold silk on pink satin*** and carry with you. It may also be engraved on a ring or an amulet. ***Note:*** The hand holding the cross in the above talisman represents the Voodoo loa *Bade*, companion and close friend of the loa *Sogbo* (see Chapter 26). *Bade* is friendly, considerate and always ready to fight evil forces. The other symbols are simply made to intensify the power of *Bade*, and to help direct them in aiding a believer in times of dire need. This loa requires an offering of red wine and a quiet prayer in return for his services. He will otherwise refuse to take any action in your behalf.

TO WASH AWAY THE WORK OF EVIL FORCES

Rose Bark (crushed)	**2 teaspoons**
Rose Petals	**2 teaspoons**
Violet Leaves	**2 teaspoons**
Tonka Beans (crushed)	**1/2 cup**
Lavender Powder	**3 teaspoons**
AniseSeeds	**3 teaspoons**
Verbena Leaves	**1/4 cup**
Cinnamon(crushed)	**1/4 cup**
Frankincense	**2 teaspoons**
Patchouli Leaves	**1/2 cup**
Quassia Chips	**1/2 cup**

Blend all of the above ingredients in a large wooden bowl, cover tightly, and set in a cool, dark place until needed. Then just before bathing, put 1/4 cup of the mixture into a cloth bag and tie the top tightly together. Draw your bath water as hot as you can stand it and immediately drop the bag into the tub. Leave it to soak for 7 minutes. Then climb into the tub and bathe as you usually do. Upon finishing, and after drying off well, drain the tub. Lastly remove the bag, wring it out thoroughly, and quickly throw it away. A fresh bag of this mixture must be used each time you take a bath in order for the spell to remain in effect.

High Priestess Marie Comtesse is said to have been the originator of this powerful unhexing spell. Never was she seen in the streets of New Orleans without her leather satchel or white velvet bag full of her Voodoo materials. This woman made much money in her day, but she died of a broken neck after falling from a balcony. Rumors were that she had been under the influence of a rival Queen's death hex. Comtesse is said to be buried in the "Wishing Vault" of St. Louis Cemetery No. 1, the same vault in which most people think Marie Laveau is resting.

TO REVERSE THE EFFECT OF AN EVIL SPELL

This is another of Marie Laveau's extremely simple methods of breaking the power of an evil spell, and it's especially good to use on someone who is actually believed to be possessed of a bad spirit force. This ritual must only be used to assist someone of the opposite sex. All you need is 1 teaspoonful of crushed ***Wahoo Bark*** *and 1 gallon of boiling water. Blend these two ingredients in a large cast iron kettle, cover tightly, and allow it to simmer for 15 minutes. Then take the kettle from the stove and allow the mixture to cool before it is used.*

When the ***Wahoo Bark*** *liquid has cooled to lukewarm, carefully strain it through a piece of muslin. Then take a clean new sponge and soak it in the liquid. Have the victim who believes he or she is under possession immediately strip down to complete nudity. They must be naked or the spell will not take effect. Begin lightly sponging their body, starting at the head and proceeding all the way down to the toes. Be especially careful to miss no spots on the body. Get between the toes, under the arms, in the ears, and even under the foreskin of the penis if the sponging is being done to a man, or between the lips of the vagina if to a woman.*

As you sponge off the possessed victim, repeat the word "Wahoo-Wahoo" 9 times as you work the sponge lightly over the body. The spell is said to be broken as soon as the sponging has been satisfactorily completed.

Marie Laveau was a hairdresser by trade immediately after her husband, Jacques Paris, died. She worked in the homes of New Orleans most fashionable whites, and at the same time, procured young and beautiful quadroon and octoroon girls for white gentlemen. Prominent people with political influence were always invited to participate in Marie's orgies during, her long reign as High Priestess of Voodoo, and whites often outnumbered the blacks in attendance. She still lived in her St. Ann Street cottage in 1875 but was never then seen in public. Marie was about 85 years old when she finally died on June 24, 1881.

26

To Avoid Mistakes

TO KEEP FROM MAKING MISTAKES

This powerful talisman will help its possessor avoid making serious errors in judgement. It is a wonderful aid when figures are being calculated, when a marriage is being planned, or for any other important undertaking. You will be protected against failure and unnecessary antagonisms. Embroider in ***black silk on white satin*** and carry with you. It may also be engraved on a ring or an amulet. ***Note:*** The black storm cloud with the lightning bolt represents the Voodoo loa *Sogbo,* who is said to throw down polished stones from the heavens. When found, these stones are considered to be sacred. *Sogbo is* known to be the inseparable companion of the loa *Bade* (Chapter 25), another protective spirit. The other symbols are simply made to assist *Sogbo* in directing his powerful forces when called upon to do so. He requires an offering of one spool of white cotton thread before he will unleash his forces in your behalf.

TO ELIMINATE MISTAKES IN LOVE

This powerful ancient charm was created in the twelfth century and made popular by Voodoo practitioners in the United States many years ago. It is known for its ability to help those who are prone to making serious mistakes in their choice of lovers and mates.

Take a small piece of clean parchment paper, and with ***Dove's Blood Ink,*** draw the following:

```
O P N S X D T
  P N S X D T
    N S X D T
      S X D T
        X D T
          D T
            T
```

When the ink dries, fold the paper over a number of times, and carry it in a pocket of a purse. But remember to never be without it. Then go outside at midnight and sprinkle a little ***Jinx Removing Salt*** all around the house. Be especially careful to get by all windows and doors. No one must be allowed to see you do this. Now return to the house and go to bed in safety.

Before entertaining a prospective lover, bathe in hot water to which you have added some ***Jinx Removing Oil.*** Then when your new love arrives, burn some ***Jinx Removing Incense*** in the room as you talk about everything. Express your feelings openly and try to appear rather uninhibited.

If lovemaking does eventually take place during the course of the evening, be sure to first anoint a ***Red Candle*** and set it close to the bed. Use ***Protection Oil*** for this purpose. Lastly, just before initiating a sexual act, rub yourself down with **Attraction *Oil*** and ***Protection Oil.*** Have intercourse or other forms of sexual activity only by the flickering light of the candle.

TO CANCEL THE EFFECT OF A MISTAKE

Untold amounts of mental torture are often the end result of a serious mistake. When you fully realize the consequences of your mistakes, this charm may be created to cast a special spell of protection. It renders others helpless to take advantage of your errors and will stop them from hurting you or others who may have fallen victim of something you have thoughtlessly done. Begin developing this charm on an evening when there is a full moon. You will need the following ingredients:

Van Van Floor Wash	**1 bottle**
War Powder	**1 packet**
Helping Hand Incense	**1 packet**
John the Conqueror Incense	**1 packet**
Black Candle	**1**
War Water	**1 bottle**
Confusion Powder	**1 packet**

Start by scrubbing your floor with hot water to which the ***Van Van Floor Wash*** has been added. This step must be repeated every third day for at least 2 weeks.

Then sprinkle some of the ***War Powder*** across the front of your yard and especially by all doors and windows. Now wait 3 days, and on the third morning burn equal amounts of ***Helping Hand Incense* and *John the Conqueror Incense,*** on a plain white saucer, in the middle of your living room. Each night, exactly at sunset, light the ***Black Candle*** and let it burn until you go to bed.

On the fourth day, take the ***War Water*** and sprinkle this all around your front yard. Then sprinkle quite a bit of the ***Confusion Powder*** on your front door.

This famous ritual was used by the well known Doctor Jack, mentioned previously, who was a powerful High Priest of Voodoo in New Orleans during the 1850's and 1860's. This man was in great demand for years and many of his faithful followers believed him to be infallible. He never charged less than $20 for his services. Doctor Jack died on June 10, 1869, from fear of one of his own charms - this one a perfumed beef heart hanging over his bed. He was convinced that when it fell off he would face certain death. One night the beef heart did fall. He awoke with a start, went into shock, and passed away in 3 days. Those who knew him best said he actually went insane.

TO ELIMINATE ERRORS IN JUDGEMENT

Take a small piece of ***Queen Elizabeth Root*** and tie one end of a 12 inch string around it. This is to be used as a potent pendulum whenever you seek answers to important questions. Rest your elbow on a table and hold the string between your thumb and forefinger. Allow the ***Queen Elizabeth Root*** to dangle close to but not actually touching the table. Ask aloud any question to which you desire an answer. Continue repeating the question until the root begins to move. If it swings away from you the answer is said to be "no." But should the root swing from right to left, the answer is said to be "yes."

This old method of divination is believed to answer with an uncanny degree of accuracy. It will help anyone who has a problem with errors of judgement. Blacks in Louisiana used it regularly during the early period of our history. ***Queen Elizabeth Root*** is still popular in all areas of the United States where Voodoo is practiced. One current Voodoo Queen in the Mississippi Delta region swears by it. She uses this particular root for assisting other people in time of need, to gain answers regarding the future, and for other purposes as well. This black lady has a fantastic reputation in her area as a woman not to cross. Her conjure bags are more powerful than any other Voodoo practitioners in that section of the country.

27

To Be Immune to Danger

DOC HENRY'S WAY TO AVOID DANGEROUS SITUATIONS

This powerful charm is said, by Doctor Henry Duplantier, to be wonderful for washing away malignant forces which may be propelling you towards danger. You will need the following ingredients:

Voodoo or Uncrossing Wash	**1 bottle**
UncrossingPowder	**1 packet**
Helping Hand Incense	**1 packet**
Black&RedDoubleActionCandle	**1**
White Protection Candle	**1**

Upon arising each morning, take a warm or hot bath. Add 1 teaspoon of ***Voodoo Wash*** to the water as you get in the tub. Soak for about 15 minutes, then get out, dry off thoroughly, and sprinkle your body well with ***Uncrossing Powder.***

At sunset each evening, light some of the ***Helping Hand Incense*** and the ***Black & Red Double Action Candle.*** Sit in complete solitude and concentrate on the situation you feel is of grave danger to you. Think of the problem being overcome and then disappearing. After you have meditated enough, say aloud the following invocation:

Here is what I fear most O good spirits!
Things look bad for me and how well I know this!
The danger is like a giant not to be overcome!
Yet, I will conquer it—I will—I will!

Lastly, light the ***white candle,*** walk slowly around the room with it, and say aloud:

You are my courage, strength and fortitude!
You will assist me in achieving victory!
My enemy is defeated, danger leaves me!
The battle is won, the end is in sight!

Extinguish both the black & red and the white candles when you have completed these invocations. Before going tc sleep, read ***Psalm 36*** which tells of man's wicked ways, and then ***Psalm 35*** which is a prayer requesting aid for those in trouble. This entire ritual is to be repeated for 3 consecutive nights.

Doc Duplantier or Doctor Henry was a Voodoo King of high regard around 1900. Not much is known about his activities except that he was once sued by a woman he had placed a curse upon. He was taken to court in 1902 and lightly fined. Henry continued his practice for a short time after this but soon disappeared and was not heard from again.

TO PROTECT YOU FROM ALL DANGER

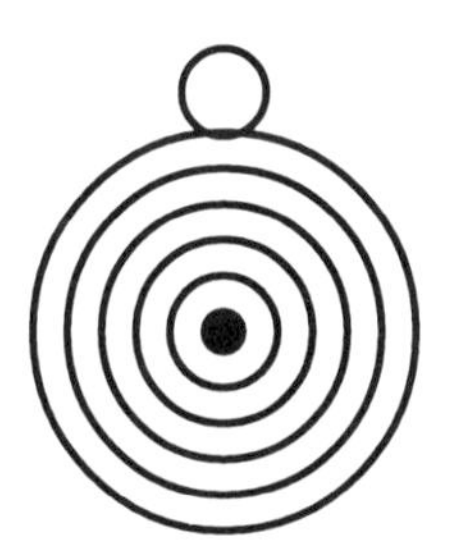

This wonderful talisman is one of the most powerful protective devices known in Voodoo today. It thwarts danger at every turn. Never will its owner be harmed by evil forces of the spirit world or machinations of enemies in the physical world. Embroider in ***light brown silk on yellow satin*** and carry with you. It may also be engraved on a ring or an amulet. ***Note:*** The series of circles within a circle represents the Voodoo loa *Salango,* guardian of all people who are in any danger. *Salango* is extremely dependable when called upon to help. An offering of cooked red beans is necessary to gain the favor and undivided attention of this loa. Place these beans in a colorful bowl and set near a door or window of the house. If you fail to do this, no action will be taken in your behalf.

TO WARD OFF DANGEROUS ILLNESSES

Get a ***small red flannel bag or a chamois sack*** and put the following ingredients into it:

Lodestone	**1 pair**
Seal of Spiritual Assistance	**1**
Seal of Spirits	**1**
Helping Hand Incense	**1 teaspoon**
Confusion Powder	**1 teaspoon**

Sew the bag tightly together and put it in your purse or pocket, whichever the case may be. Or you may wear it around your neck on a string or a chain. The **2 *Lodestones*** are very important in this amulet. One is believed to attract the forces of good, while the other repels the evil spirits. Wear or carry this bag faithfully whenever you leave the house, and when people are visiting.

You may also wish to carry a ***Carbuncle*** with you as this is said to build confidence in times of need, and it helps draw healing spirits when you are confronted by any kind of disease or illness.

This is another of the famous Rockford Lewis charms. In 1934 when only 29 years old and already fantastically wealthy as a result of his thriving Voodoo business, the roof fell in. Lewis was arraigned in Federal court on a mail fraud charge. Rockford simply denied having anything to do with Voodoo, and was quoted by the *New Orleans Item* as saying: "I handles medals, sachet bags, lucky beans, lucky medals. Yes, sir, I believes in luck. I believes in helping people. But mostly I handles 'Save Your Life Rheumatic Oil.' I sells a lot of that." He was subsequently convicted and sentenced to spend 2 years in the Federal Penitentary at Atlanta, Georgia.

TO STOP A DANGEROUS LOVER

This special protective charm was designed years ago by Doctor John in order to prevent an angry lover from instigating a scandal over an illicit affair. It has worked wonders for hundreds of people in the past.

Low John the Conqueror Root	**1 piece**
Helping Hand Incense	**1 packet**

Carry some bits of ***Low John the Conqueror Root*** with you wherever you happen to go. A small piece is to be dropped on the front step of the house in which your revenge-minded lover resides. This act alone is believed to silence the lips of that person from spreading rumors about you. Also read aloud Psalm 52 each morning upon arising. Then burn a little ***Helping Hand Incense*** daily during the following Mars hours:

Sunday	**2:00 pm and 8:00 pm**
Monday	**6:00 pm and 10;00 pm**
Tuesday	**3:00 pm and 9:00 pm**
Wednesday	**7:00 pm and 11:00 pm**
Thursday	**4:00 pm and 7:00 pm**
Friday	**1:00 pm and 6:00 pm**
Saturday	**5:00 pm and Midnight**

All your thoughts and deeds and actions should be above criticism. You must not enter into gossip about your former loved one or even speak critically of him or her. Make no remarks of a derogatory nature about the person. Follow the above instructions carefully and your infuriated ex-lover will be silenced. Only joy will enter your life from this point on.

Voudou John, or more commonly called Doctor John, had many important people for clients. One famous customer of his was Pauline, a mulatto. She was the first person ever to be hanged (March 28, 1846) in Parish Prison. In *New Orleans as it Was*, Henry C. Castellanos writes in reference to John's thousands of white followers: *"One would stand aghast were he told the names of the high society dames, who were wont to drive to this sooty black Cagliostro's abode, to consult him upon domestic affairs."*

28

To Make Yourself Sensual

TO AROUSE DESIRE IN THE OPPOSITE SEX

This fabulous talisman incites sexual feelings in others whenever you happen to come near. It helps the wearer to better understand a prospective lovemaking partner and reveals important clues to assist in a conquest. Embroider in ***silver silk on light blue satin*** and carry with you. It may also be engraved on a ring or an amulet. ***Note:*** The bent stemmed flower represents the Voodoo loa *Ezili*, goddess of voluptuousness and femininity. She makes the wearer exude sexuality and magnetism. *Ezili* not only causes arousal in the person who wears this talisman. She also creates unexpected sexual urges in anyone of the opposite sex you come into contact with. This goddess is known as a specialist in oral sex and she induces others to partake in this form of lovemaking. To make a female lover perform fellatio, or a male lover perform cunnilingus, simply whisper the words *Patchouly, Mooga, Karenga, Desular*, during preliminary petting. *Ezili* requires an offering of menstrual blood and semen, blended well, before she will take any action in your behalf.

TO HELP STIMULATE PASSION

The formation used in making the letter "Y" is considered to be a symbol representing life to Voodooists. It was brought into popularity by New Orleans's first recorded Voodoo Queen, Sanite Dede. Engrave this letter on a square ring, charm, or anything you regularly carry with you. It is said to stimulate those of the opposite sex, increase your sexual magnetism, protect from venereal diseases, and attract experienced lovers. This talisman also helps the possessor to gain clairvoyant power.

High Priestess Sanite Dede was widely known in her day for the interracial Voodoo ceremonies she held. Dede was famous for her love and sex charms as well as for her power of hexing. In *Metropolitan Life Unveiled, J. W.* Buel describes one of her rituals as follows: "Each man and woman had a white handkerchief tied around the forehead.... There were males and females, old and young, and handsome mulatresses and quadroons. With them half a dozen white men and two white women...."

TO GAIN SENSUALITY

A roving mate or lover, according to High Priestess Malvina Latour, can be easily made to stay at home if these simple instructions are carried out. You will become more sensually appealing than ever before. Blend the following ingredients:

Lavender Flowers	**1 teaspoon**
Witch's Grass	**2 teaspoons**
Wood Betany Root	**2 teaspoons**

Violet Leaves	**1 teaspoon**
Genital Hairs	**7**

Place this mixture in ***7 separate red flannel bags***. Be sure that 1 genital hair goes in each bag. Sew the tops of the bags. Put 1 under your bed, 1 under the mattress, and 1 in your pillow case. The other 4 are to go in each corner of your bedroom. Then sprinkle your naked body with ***Sensuality Oil*** and powder your genitals with ***Attraction Powder.*** Your love partner will become exceedingly amorous over your sexual magnetism. He or she will never desire anyone more than they do you. Your physical allure will be irresistible.

Queen Latour was a powerful Voodoo High Priestess during the late 1800's, yet she didn't seem to have the compelling personality of the former Queen, Marie Laveau. The stringent control over all Voodoo cult activities began to disintegrate under this woman's leadership. Many rival Queens quickly came on the scene and started challenging her authority. Voodoo Doctors or High Priests for the first time dared to assume duties formerly reserved only for the Queens when Marie Laveau ruled so supremely and unquestioned.

SENSUAL HOURS TO CAPITALIZE UPON

Marie Laveau, the most powerful Voodoo Queen in New Orleans' history, believed that the highest degree of sensuality always began when the moon was waxing. She advised her clients to let the hours of Venus be their guide to becoming more of a truly sensual person, one who inflames the passions of others at a glance or a light touch.

Plan all of your sexual activities, dates and even casual meetings according to the following table. But, before going out, put 2 teaspoons of ***Sensuous Bath Oil*** in a tub of lukewarm bath water. Bathe slowly, then carefully dry off, and rub your body lightly with some ***Love Powder.*** Dress and lastly sprinkle a little of this same powder on your clothing.

Marie Laveau was extremely well known for her powerful love potions, charms and amulets, as well as for her other Voodoo sorcery. Her rituals were often described in the local newspapers. On June 28, 1872, a *New Orleans Times* reporter wrote about one of her St. John's Eve Voodoo rituals. He said it was no more than an orgy and that "the people were about equally divided male and female - a few more females. The larger portion of the crowd Negroes and quadroons, but about one hundred whites, say thirty or forty men, the remainder women."

TABLE OF THE HOURS OF SENSUALITY

Sunday	***2:00 pm and 9:00 pm***
	4:00 pm and 11:00 pm
Monday	***6:00 am***
	1:00 pm and 8:00 pm
Tuesday	***3:00 am and 10:00 am***
	5:00 pm and Midnight
Wednesday	***7:00 am***
	2:00 pm and 9:00 pm
Thursday	***4:00 am and 11:00 am***
	6:00 pm
Friday	***1:00 am and 8:00 am***
	3:00 pm and 11:00 pm
Saturday	***5:00 am and Noon***
	7:00 pm

29

To Find New Sexual Partners

FORTUNATE DAYS FOR FINDING LOVERS

Many factors were believed, by High Priestess Marie Saloppe, to influence the search for new sexual partners. One should try to attract good vibrations in every way possible. Certain days are reputed to be more sexually attracting for different persons. According to ancient Voodoo lore, it is best to engage in a search for sexual activity and experiences on these days:

YOUR ASTROLOGICAL SIGN	*TRY THIS DAY*
Capricorn	**Monday & Thursday**
Cancer	**Tuesday & Saturday**
Pisces	**Wednesday & Monday**
Libra	**Thursday & Sunday**
Sagittarius	**Friday & Wednesday**
Scorpio	**Saturday & Tuesday**
Leo	**Monday & Saturday**
Taurus	**Tuesday & Friday**
Virgo	**Wednesday & Monday**
Aries	**Thursday & Friday**
Aquarius	**Friday & Wednesday**
Gemini	**Saturday & Tuesday**

Marie Saloppe, High Priestess in New Orleans of the 1820's, was placed under a terrible curse by Marie Laveau. She soon lost all of her tremendous power and fast became an old crone of a street character. She then went under the name of Zozo LaBrique. This demented creature ended up selling buckets of brick dust for 5 cents each. Brick dust was popular in those days for scrubbing the front steps of homes as it was believed to have the power of scrubbing away evil spirits.

TO MAKE SOMEONE DESIRE YOU SEXUALLY

This talisman opens all hearts upon first meeting. Others will immediately become sex-minded and want to go to bed with the wearer. Suggestions for lovemaking should be bold and numerous. Embroider in ***silver silk on deep-blue satin*** and carry with you. It may also be engraved on a ring or an amulet. ***Note:*** The smiling sun denotes the Voodoo loa *Mystere*, goddess of lust, passion and sensuality. She induces those of the opposite sex to desire you passionately, and to be more openly frank about their sexual feelings and needs. The two eyes are said to open the mind of anyone who touches or even looks upon this talisman. The black square figure generates sensuality and forces a sexual partner to desire you even more. The other symbols help to concentrate the sensuality of *Mystere* and thereby direct her power more accurately. This loa requires an offering of peppered apple juice before she will take any action on your behalf. Another talisman utilizing the power *of Mystere* can be found in Chapter 13.

WHEN SEXUAL DESIRE FOR SOMEONE IS A SECRET

The following ingredients are to be carefully blended. When finished, place the mixture in a ***red flannel bag*** and tightly tie the top together. Attach a ***white cotton string*** and wear around your neck. Within 7 days your wish for a new sexual partner will be fulfilled.

(continued)

Camphor Powder	***1/2 teaspoon***
Frankincense	***1 teaspoon***
Myrrh Incense	***A pinch***
Orris Root Powder	***1/4 teaspoon***
Patchouly Leaves (ground)	***A pinch***
Sandalwood Incense	***1/4 teaspoon***
Saltpeter	***3/4 teaspoon***

If you do not obtain a new lover within the 7 day period, empty the sack. Burn a small amount of the mixture each morning for 7 straight days. You will unexpectedly meet and make passionate love with someone.

Marie Laveau, who ruled all Voodoo in New Orleans from the 1820's to 1869, was the originator of the above love charm. She was said to be expert in all things supernatural: The *New Orleans Democrat* of June 18, 1881, reported on her as follows: "She was, up to an advanced age, the prime mover and soul of the indecent orgies of the ignoble Voudous; and to her influence may be attributed the fall of many a virtuous woman."

DON PEDRO'S METHOD OF GAINING A SPECIAL LOVER

Pink Candle	**1**
Helping Hand Incense	***1 packet***

Light the ***Pink Candle*** and let it burn for 7 full minutes each day at sunset. The candle should be carefully placed on a saucer or some flat dish. Arrange 7 small pebbles around the bottom of the candle. Each pebble should be marked with the initials of one person you desire sexually. Stare at the pebbles as the candle burns and drips. The pebble first touched by the melted wax denotes the man or woman you should concentrate on having relations with.

Now light some ***Helping Hand Incense*** and close your eyes. Begin to visualize your lover in the nude. Concentrate for at least 10 minutes. Then write a friendly note to that person. Arrange for a meeting as soon as practical. Sexual relations will take place within 2 weeks, if not sooner.

Keep in mind that this spell works only for those who realize an affair will last as long as they are honest about their feelings. You must also agree to be faithful during the period of the sexual relationship. This as well as physical intercourse must be freely given your loved one.

This potent spell is another of the fantastic creations of the great love specialist in Voodoo of 1800 New Orleans. One of Don Pedro's interracial orgies (of which there were a multitude) was described in this way by one observer during a police raid: "The most degrading and infamous feature of this scene was the presence of a very large number of ladies (?), moving in the highest walks of society, rich and hitherto supposed respectable, that were caught in the dragnet. Two of them, through consideration for the feelings of their relatives and connections, so unexpectedly brought to shame, were permitted to escape, while the husband of a third, unable to survive the disgrace of his wife, deliberately took his life on the following day. These facts were the subject of gossip for many a year."

BEST TIME FOR CASTING SEXUAL SPELLS

Voodoo High Priestess Betsy Toledano agreed with Marie Laveau's basic premise that sexual spells are much more powerful when undertaken during the waxing of the moon. She did not agree with Laveau as to the exact hours and she then went a step further and recommended you use the following items:

Attraction Oil	**1 bottle**
Adam and Eve Root	**1 pair**

Decide when to start casting your sexual attraction spell by carefully consulting the table given below. Upon selecting the proper hour to begin, write a note to the one you desire. Sprinkle it liberally with ***Attraction Oil*** and wrap it around the ***Adam and Eve Root.*** Carry this with you at all times and you will be making love within a few short weeks.

TABLE OF SEXUAL ATTRACTING-HOURS

DAY	TIME—AM	TIME—PM
Sunday	2:00 and 8:00	3 00 and 10:00
Monday	6:00 and 9:00	2:00 and 7:00
Tuesday	3:00 and 7:00	6:00 and 11:00

DAY	TIME—AM	TIME—PM
Wednesday	5:00 and 11:00	1:00and 8:00
Thursday	1:00 and 10:00	5:00 and 10:30
Friday	4:00 and 6.00	4:00 and 10:00
Saturday	5:00 and 10:30	2:00 and 6:00

Betsy Toledano was another legendary Voodoo Queen in New Orleans during the 1850's. She was described in one newspaper account as a "stout and intelligent free woman of color." This conjure lady claimed to have inherited the right to rule without police interference in her Voodoo activities. According to another newspaper, Betsy was a sincere practitioner and "contended she had a perfect right to hold meetings of the Voudou Society . . . that the Society was a religious institution which had been transmitted to her, through her grandmother and mother, from the ancient Congo Queens."

30

To Increase Business

TO ATTRACT NEW BUSINESS

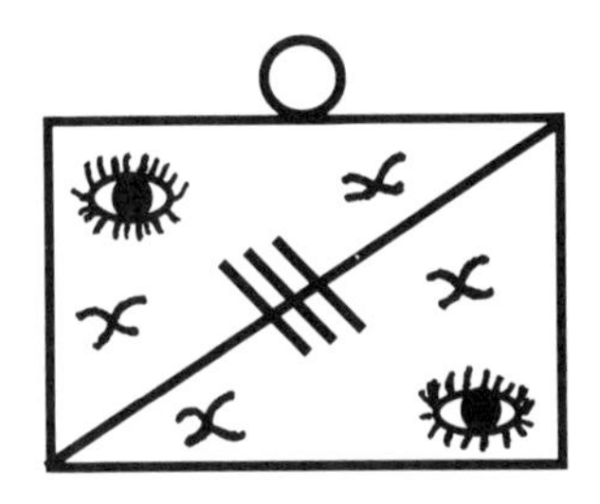

This unusual talisman is ideal for making a business more profitable. It was used in early American Voodoo practice by numerous prostitutes in an attempt to attract new customers, and to increase the amount paid for sexual services. Customers coming in once were said to surely return with friends if this talisman were worn during intercourse, or kept under the pillow. Embroider in ***gray silk on black satin*** and carry with you. It may also be engraved on a ring or amulet. ***Note:*** The two eyes in the above talisman represent the all encompassing vision and power of the Voodoo loa *Ezili-Mapyang,* protector of prostitutes and other business enterprises. The other symbols are simply made to intensify the power off this spirit force. *Ezili-Mapyang* always requires an offering of 7 copper pennies placed in a circle around a pink candle. Without this offering she will refuse to take any action on your behalf.

TO BRING NEW CUSTOMERS

John the Conqueror Root	**1 piece**
Red Clover Powder	**1 teaspoon**
BroomTopHerb(powdered)	**1 teaspoon**
Money Oil	**1 bottle**
Squill Powder	**1/2 cup**
Sea Salt	**2/3 cup**
Money Drawing Incense	**2 packet**
John the Conqueror Incense	**2 packets**

Put the ***John the Conqueror Root*** in a small chamois bag with the ***Red Clover Powder, Broom Top Herb*** and 7 drops of ***Money Oil.*** Tie the bag tightly shut with green cotton thread and carry it with you every hour of the business day. Sprinkle the bag with 7 more drops of ***Money Oil,*** every seventh day to make it regain its original strength. Do not lose this bag under any circumstances!

Now blend the ***Squill Powder, Sea Salt and 1 gallon of rain water.*** Pour it into a large crock or jug, shake well, cover tightly, and stand in a cool dark place for a period of 7 days. Then strain the mixture through muslin and sprinkle a little of it on the floor of your business place, every morning before opening to the public.

Lastly, blend the ***Money Drawing Incense*** and the ***John the Conqueror Incense.*** Burn 1/2 teaspoon each morning in your place of business before opening for the day. Read aloud ***Psalm 114*** as the incense smolders.

This potent ritualistic charm is credited to the Voodoo High Priest who practiced under the name of Nathan Barnes, Doctor Barnes, and even Doc Nathan. He started his Voodoo work in 1880 and was still going strong as late as 1944, then 85 years old. Barnes made a good living from his Voodoo business and said he did only good things for people. This man swore he had never placed a curse on anyone.

TO HAVE A SUCCESSFUL SALE

John the Conqueror Incense	2 teaspoons
Echinacea Powder	1 teaspoon
Allspice	1 teaspoon
Clove	1/3 teaspoon
Bay	1/3 teaspoon
Angelica	1/3 teaspoon
Yellow Seven Day Candle	1
Most Powerful Hand Talisman	1
Money Attraction Oil	1 bottle

Blend the first 4 ingredients together in a small wooden bowl, cover tightly, and store in a dark corner of a closet. Burn a little of this mixture each morning upon arising (preferably at sunrise) and each evening at sunset. Do this for a minimum of 7 days prior to the start of any sale. Also burn the ***Yellow Seven Day Candle*** during this same time period. Each morning, as the incense smolders, read aloud ***Psalm 4.*** Then on the morning of the sale, anoint the ***Most Powerful Hand Talisman*** with some of the ***Money Attraction Oil.*** Wear the talisman around your neck or carry it in one of your pockets or purse.

If all of the above instructions are faithfully carried out to the letter, a successful sale is said to be guaranteed. You will make large profits and gain a multitude of new customers as well as a host of good friends.

This old Voodoo charm is also said to induce those who come to your sale to purchase much more than planned. It opens the purse strings of misers and spendthrifts. The charm was developed and used in the 1880's by an old woman called Helen Thomas, who proclaimed it would do much for hapless prostitutes in need of new customers. This crone was once feared as a Voodoo Queen of some standing in her day. She had a large following of white women who came and participated in her sensual rituals. Helen Thomas, as did many other High Priestesses, climaxed her ceremonies with a promiscuous sex orgy in which whites and blacks freely mingled and mated in abandonment.

31

To Stop a Wandering Lover

TO MAKE YOUR LOVER DESIRE ONLY YOU

This long secret mixture of love incense was created by the great New Orleans love doctor of Voodoo, Don Pedro, between 1840 and 1890. It was said to be guaranteed to raise the penis of any man and to wet the vaginal lips of any woman who was subjected to its spell. It increases the sexual charms of the person mixing and burning it. By using this incense at night, while making love, your partner will quickly lose all interest in others. In fact, a woman who does run around, will become frigid when she is in bed with another man. A man who has affairs on the side will be unable to achieve an erection while in the presence and arms of some other woman. You will need the following ingredients:

Sandalwood Incense	**1/2 cup**
Lavender Flowers(crushed)	**1/2 cup**
Bayberry Herb(crushed)	**2 cups**
Cinnamon Powder	**1/4 cup**
Paradise Grains (crushed)	**1/4 cup**
Tobacco	**2 teaspoons**
Gilead Buds (crushed)	**1 cup**
Violet Powder	**1/4 cup**
Allspice	**2 teaspoons**
Verbena Leaves (crushed)	**1/4 cup**
Saltpeter	**1/2 teaspoon**

Blend all of the above ingredients in a large wooden bowl and tightly cover when not being used. This special love incense must be well mixed or it will not accomplish the desired end results.

A small amount should be burned at least 3 times daily in order to increase the sensual vibrations all throughout your place of residence.

Don Pedro was not a man to take lightly. He was feared and highly respected in early New Orleans Voodoo circles. This man claimed to be a "healer," but was in fact, a specialist in love and sexual charms. He was arrested numerous times, when his large scale interracial orgies were raided, but seemed always to come out of it unscathed. After one raid, Don Pedro pleaded his case before the judge and claimed he was merely "treating all the naked participants for rheumatism."

TO PREVENT INFIDELITY

This popular talisman is commonly used to stop a lover or a mate from having a secret affair. It stymies an illicit relationship and causes sexual problems to arise between the wayward couple. It makes the possessor of the talisman more appealing than ever before in the past. Embroider in ***lilac silk on deep purple satin*** and carry with you. It may also be engraved on a ring or an amulet.

Note: The man with the limp, lightning struck penis symbolizes the Voodoo loa *Gran Erzalie.* This loa always helps those with troubled marriages and single people with problem love affairs. She is also known for her kindly assistance to prostitutes who call on her for guidance. Gran Erzalie requires an offering of fresh semen on a plain white handkerchief or napkin. The semen must be that from the man who is being unfaithful, or whose lover is having sexual relations with another man. Without such an offering, this loa will refuse to take any action on your behalf.

TO BREAK YOUR LOVER'S OTHER SEXUAL RELATIONSHIP

This old Voodoo charm was designed by High Priestess Sanite Dede to force a lover to immediately stop having sexual relations with others. It is a powerful method of wreaking vengeance on someone who has deeply hurt you by entering into an illicit affair. It is said not only to make your partner unable to have sex while away from you but it also creates dangerous animosity between wayward lovers. Use this charm with great caution. You will need the following ingredients:

Black Jumbo Candle	**1**
Cowgrass	**1 teaspoon**
Rosemary (crushed)	**1 teaspoon**
Pine Herb (crushed)	**1 teaspoon**
Red Wax (melted)	**1 teaspoon**

First, light the ***Black Jumbo Candle*** and melt it completely down. Then take a ***small piece of parchment paper*** and write the name of your lover. Press this paper deeply into the still soft candle wax, roll into a neat ball, and set aside in a dark closet to harden. Meanwhile, carefully line a ***small cardboard box*** with the ***Cowgrass.*** When the black wax ball has sufficiently hardened, place it in the center of the box. Sprinkle the ball with the ***Rosemary and Pine Herb.*** Carefully fit the lid on the box, tie with ***white cotton string,*** and seal all 4 corners with the melted ***Red Wax.*** Set the box aside for 3 days. Then take it to any place with running water (a river, stream, etc.) and toss it in. Turn away and return home. Do not look back or the charm will lose all its power. Mama Dede as she was often called by followers, was believed to be one of the best when it came to preparing love charms. She used live snakes in her rituals and employed sex as a major ingredient. A part of one of her rituals was once described as follows: "Under the passion of the hour, the women tore off their garments, and entirely nude, went on dancing, but wriggling like snakes.... The orgies became frightful. Suddenly the candles flared up and went out, leaving nothing but a faint glow from the dying pyres."

TO INCREASE YOUR SEXUAL CHARM

Pimento Powder	**1 teaspoon**
Bayberry Incense	**1/2 cup**
Orchid (crushed)	**1/2 cup**
Frankincense Powder	**1/4 cup**
Dill	**1/4 cup**

Blend all of the above ingredients in a wooden bowl, cover tightly, and set aside in a cool dark place until needed. It is to be burned on ***Fast Lighting Charcoal.*** Burn a small amount of the mixture just before your loved one is due home, and also burn more while in the throes of passionate lovemaking. Your lover will appreciate you more fully as a result of this, and he or she will cease having sexual relations with others.

This charm is credited to Marie Laveau, a woman who helped thousands of Creole ladies in their *affaires d'amour.* In *New Orleans as it Was,* Castellanos reports: "Her apartments were often thronged with visitors from every class and section, in search of aid from her supposed supernatural powers. Ladies of high social position would frequently pay her high prices for amulets...." Marie Laveau died in 1881, a feeble, quaking old woman with a shriveled, yellowish neck and gray tresses hanging in terrible disarray about her head. Of interest is the fact that when at her zenith as Queen, Marie Leveau never received less than $500 for her unhexing services, and her fee often ran as high as $1000. People waited in line to see her!

32

To Protect Your Children

TO PROTECT YOUR CHILDREN

This wonderful talisman has special protective qualities which will work only on children. Each child in the family should be given one at birth. It should be placed on a chain or string around the neck and never taken off. The good spirit forces are said to be drawn to the child and they will strive to keep it out of trouble. It will protect against all forms of illness; and help the child to excel. Embroider in green silk on yellow satin. It may also be engraved on a ring or an amulet. *Note:* The tadpole in the above talisman represents the Voodoo loa Agwe-Taroyo, guardian of all children in trouble. The other symbols are simply made to help intensify her powers and to direct them when she is called upon for assistance. Agwe-Taroyo requires an offering of a child's favorite toy placed between 2 burning white candles. She will not take any action in your child's behalf until such an offering is made.

TO BE CERTAIN YOUR CHILD IS ALWAYS SAFE

Planet Mars Talisman	1
Fast Luck Oil	1 bottle
Woodruff	1 packet
Mugwort(crushed)	1 packet
Master of Woods Powder	1 packet

You will need all of the above materials before starting to create this powerful protection charm and spell. First take the ***Planet Mars Talisman*** and anoint it with 7 drops of ***Fast Luck Oil.*** The child should be made to wear this talisman around his or her neck at all times. It is best to hang it on a good chain to prevent it getting lost while out playing. The talisman must again be anointed every seventh day with 7 more drops of ***Fast Luck Oil.***

Next, put some ***Master of the Woods Powder*** in a small ***red flannel bag,*** tie the top together tightly, and hide it under the child's mattress.

Lastly, sprinkle equal amounts of ***Woodruff and Mugwort*** in any dresser drawers and closets used for storing your child's, clothing.

According to Marie Comtesse, if you faithfully follow all of these directions, your home will be blessed, and your children will always be carefully watched over. Queen Comtesse, sometimes known as Mama Comtesse or Mama Marie, used this protective device quite often in the late 1800's. She was especially noted for her showmanship and used only young and beautiful, scantily clad or nude mulattos to dance at her suggestive, sexually oriented rituals. And these young females (usually still in their teens) were also made to take part in the orgies which climaxed the ceremonies. Mama's rituals were widely advertised by word of mouth, and they always attracted many white and black men of means. They paid extremely high fees in order to attend, as there was always a multitude of sensuous, light skinned beauties who were guaranteed to satisfy every conceivable sexual need.

TO OVERCOME ANY TROUBLE YOUR CHILD HAS

Motherwort Powder	**1 oz.**
Hops Powder	**1 oz.**
Jasmine Powder	**1 oz.**
Skullcap Powder	**1 oz.**
Black Cohosh Powder	**1 oz.**
Catnip Powder	**1 oz.**
Peppermint Powder	**1 oz.**

Blend the above ingredients in a wooden bowl, cover tightly, and set aside in a cool, dark closet until needed. This mixture can be concocted yourself, from the above ingredients, or you can simply purchase the same thing already blended called ***Holy Herbs.*** It is much better to mix your own as it is said to be more potent.

Now take the blended mixture and stir it into 1 gallon of boiling water. Let it steep for at least 1 hour, or until lukewarm. Then pour into a large jug, cap tightly, and store in a cool, dark place until used.

Put 1 tablespoon of this liquid in the child's bath water every time he or she bathes. Also sprinkle a little of it in each corner of every room in the house both for further protection and as a spiritual aid.

The above charm is a creation of the notorious Doctor Cat the man considered to have been the pioneer in the field of mail-order Voodoo. Cat sold his wares all over the United States but was finally charged by the Federal Government with using the mails to defraud. He immediately left his wife and blew town with a teenage lover. Cat was eventually picked up in Birmingham, Alabama in 1914 and was also charged under the *Mann Act.* Doctor Cat looked to be about 30 years old, but he seriously claimed to be 127. He spent 2 years in prison, was subsequently divorced by his wife, and later disappeared, never to be seen or heard of again.

TO KEEP A CHILD HEALTHY

Horehound	**1/4 teaspoon**
Ash Leaves	**1/2 teaspoon**
Holy Herbs	**1/2 teaspoon**

Blend the above ingredients and then immediately add them to 1 quart of boiling water. When the water becomes lukewarm, pour it into a plain white bowl and set it in the child's room, after the sun goes down. Wait until the child goes to sleep and then lightly anoint his or her forehead with some of the water. Leave the bowl in the room for 7 full days. Then throw the mixture out and make a fresh batch. Strong healing vibrations are said to be attracted to this mixture. It protects the child from all types of trouble as well as sicknesses.

This concoction was devised in the late 1850's by Mama Antoine, New Orleans High Priestess of Voodoo. She always worked out of her house on Dumaine Street, claimed to be only a "healer," but held numerous sex orgies. Antoine and Marie Laveau worked together for a short time. They were close friends and jointly held many rituals every Monday night at Mama's house. These were the sensuous rituals at which Regina Nicaud, a later High Priestess, got her start in Voodoo as a nude dancer and sex plaything.

33

To Break a Marriage

TO ATTRACT SOMEONE ELSE'S MATE

If you should fall in love with the mate of a friend, this potent charm, created by Marie Laveau, is said to destroy the marriage. You in turn will then be the sole object of his or her affections. Blend the following ingredients:

Tonka Bean	**1 bean**
Damiana Powder	**1/2 teaspoon**
Come to Me Powder	**1 teaspoon**
7 Powers Incense	**2 teaspoons**

After all of the above materials are thoroughly mixed, put the blend in a half glass of red wine. Allow to soak for 24 hours. Then anoint yourself with this potent liquid before leaving the house. Make the sign of the cross with some of this mixture on your forehead, chest, tops of both hands and on your feet. Also sprinkle yourself with 3 drops of ***Compelling Oil.*** Dust your genital area with ***Come to Me Powder.*** Do all of these things for 21 consecutive days. After the twenty-first day, take the rest of the liquid and sprinkle it around the outer edge of your front door. The person you so strongly desire as a lover will be compelled to come and offer you love and happiness.

Marie Laveau received fantastic sums of money over the years for her services in concocting just such charms as above. She would never accept less than $10 when anyone asked her for assistance this was enough to have your fortune told and to obtain a small good luck charm or *gris gris* designed especially for whatever purpose you had in mind. Marie did much work in the area of sex during her 40 year span of rule as High Priestess in New Orleans. When an affair was wanted by someone, she charged in accordance with how wealthy a patron was and what they could afford. This type activity usually ran between $50 and $1000.

TO FORCE A MARRIAGE TO SPLIT

This excellent talisman is the one to use when you fall in love with a married man or woman. It creates animosity between the formerly happy couple and forces a hasty separation. Then the person you desire will be passionately drawn toward the possessor of the talisman. Embroider in ***light blue silk on dark blue satin*** and carry with you. It may also be engraved on a ring or an amulet.

Note: The penis pierced with a knife in the above talisman represents the vengeful loa *Guede Brave* who enjoys interfering in happy marriages and love affairs. The other symbols are simply made to help direct his powerful forces against the man or woman you wish to eliminate from the picture. Only the loa *Gran Erzalie* (Chapter 31) can overcome this loa's machinations. *Guede Brave* requires an offering of a white hen's blood before he will take any action in your behalf.

TO RUIN SOMEONE'S MARRIAGE

Impotency is the downfall of many otherwise good marriages and love relationships. Don Pedro, Voodoo King in old New Orleans, between 1840 and 1890, is reported to have carefully devised this charm. He claimed it has the power of causing the most virile of married men to be unable to gain an erection and it can make a woman totally frigid. It is according to Don Pedro, a terribly strong spell if properly carried out, and it is most difficult to break. He advised that this method should be used only as a last resort if you wish to get even with someone who has done you an injustice. You will need all of the following:

Frankincense Incense	**1/2 cup**
Cloves Powder	**1 teaspoon**
Voodoo Incense	**3 teaspoons**
Black Art Powder	**1/4 cup**
Love Breaking Incense	**3 teaspoons**
Goofer Dust	**1/4 teaspoon**

Thoroughly blend all of the above ingredients in a wooden bowl, cover tightly, and set aside in a cool dark place until needed. Then take a piece of ***parchment paper*** *and write the name of the married man or woman you wish to harm. Use only* ***Dove's Blood Ink*** *for this purpose. Carefully burn this paper by placing it in a clean white saucer with some of the incense mixture on top of it. Collect the ashes and secretly bury them behind your house. If you live in an apartment or elsewhere, bury the ashes close by but to the north of your residence. Return home and read aloud* ***Psalm 48.*** *Each day thereafter, for 10 consecutive days, burn a little of the incense mixture at both sunup and sunset. If the results do not turn out as anticipated, carefully repeat the entire procedure.*

Don Pedro reigned as supreme ruler of Voodoo in New Orleans around 1880 and 1890, although he had been involved in the practice since the 1850's. He was known as the Voodoo man to contact if you had any sexual or marital problems, yet he claimed outwardly to be nothing more than a "healer." This black man held a great number of orgies, quite a few of which were raided. One of note involved 50 people, 25 white men and 25 black and mulatto females. A wild sexual orgy was in process when the police broke it up. Cunnilingus, fellatio and intercourse in "ungodly positions" were observed, mostly in groups of 3 or more people enjoying each other in unison.

34

To Cause Insanity

TO DRIVE SOMEONE INSANE

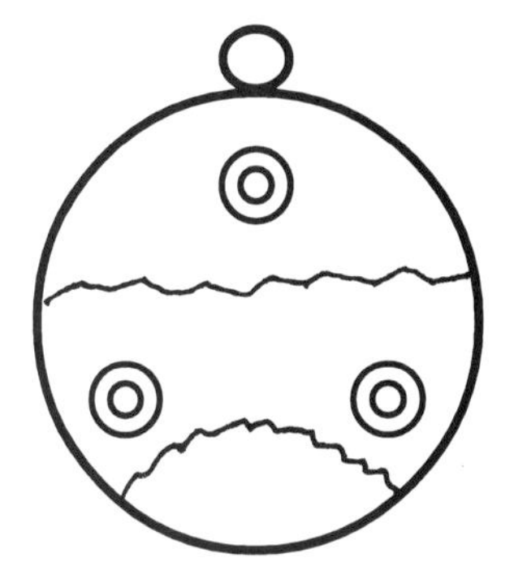

This potent talisman is the only one in Voodoo known to be used for bringing on insanity in someone the owner hates. It forces an enemy's mind to crack for no apparent reason when an injustice has been done to the person who wears the talisman. No one must ever be allowed to touch or even look upon this talisman or the effect may reverse itself and destroy its possessor. Embroider in ***cherry red silk on pink satin*** and carry with you. It may also be engraved on a ring or an amulet. ***Note:*** The three circles enclosing dots in the above talisman represent the Voodoo loa *Tii Albert*, a basically good spirit force who helps a believer drive someone out of their mind as a severe punishment for wrong doing. *Tii Albert* must be given an offering of sugar cookies before he will consent to taking any action in your behalf. Upon successful completion of his duties he must again be paid off with an offering of a bowl of hot soup. Fail to do this end you invite his wrath to turn upon you in revenge.

TO MAKE AN ENEMY GO MAD

Black Arts Incense	**1/2 cup**
Yohimbee Bark (crushed)	**1 teaspoon**
Saltpeter	**1/4 teaspoon**
Tobacco	**1 teaspoon**
Arrowroot	**1 teaspoon**
Low John Powder	**1 teaspoon**
Patchouly Powder	**2 teaspoons**
Prickly Ash Berries (crushed)	**1/2 teaspoons**

Blend all the above ingredients in a wooden bowl, cover tightly, and set aside in a cool dark place until needed. Now gather together these materials:

Black Voodoo Doll	**1**
Black Arts Oil	**1bottle**
Obeah Oil	**1 bottle**
Patchouly Oil	**1 bottle**
Black Votive Candle	**1**
Voodoo Oil	**1 bottle**
War Water	**1 bottle**

First take up the ***Black Voodoo Doll*** and sprinkle its head thoroughly with some of the ***Black Arts Oil.*** Then sprinkle the doll's body with abundant ***Obeah Oil.*** Take a piece of ***parchment paper*** and write the name of the person you wish to drive out of his or her mind. Do this 9 times with ***Dove's Blood Ink,*** or better yet, some of your own fresh blood. Attach this paper to the bottom of the doll's feet with ***9 brand new pins or needles.*** Lay the doll on a piece of ***black cotton cloth*** and liberally sprinkle it with ***Patchouly Oil.***

Now take the ***Black Votive Candle*** and carefully rub it down with ***Voodoo Oil.*** Light the candle and set it on a clean white saucer. Surround the candle with 7 small mounds of the previously prepared incense mixture. Light each mound, starting with the one furthest away from you, and proceeding in a counterclockwise direction. Allow the incense to burn itself out, but as it smolders, kneel, hold your palms open and over the ***Black Votive Candle,*** and repeat the following invocation:

By the power of Voodoo curse mine enemy!
O great Voodoo spirits drive (name) insane!
Break his mind! Break his mind!
(name) is cursed! (name) is damned!
(name) is cursed! (name) is damned!
(name) is cursed! (name) is damned!

Then soak the doll with ***War Water*** and carefully wrap it in the black cloth. Tie tightly with black thread and hide it in a dark corner where no one can possibly find it by accident.

Repeat this entire procedure with a brand new doll every 9 days. Your enemy is said to be driven insane and will stay that way so long as you continue faithfully performing this mystical ritual charm.

You can even add more power to this curse by going to your enemy's house and sprinkling the yard with ***Crossing Powder, Graveyard* Dust, and *Double Cross Powder.*** And you may even wish to sprinkle with some **Confusion *Oil, Crossing Oil, Black Arts Oil* and *Bend over Oil.***

This entire ceremony is another creation of the famous Doctor Alexander, a Voodoo "healer" in New Orleans during the 1870's and 1880's. Alexander and his wife Clemence climaxed such rituals with a performance of the sex act which they both claimed was an important part of their Voodoo work. These orgy-oriented rites were usually held at white Voodoo Queen Lou Jackson's home. In one instance, on May 28,1889, the police pulled a surprise raid on them and interrupted an orgy which was already in full swing. Two teenage girls and 13 other white women, all nude, were arrested, along with 10 nude black men. All were subsequently convicted of disorderly conduct and fined $2.50 each. Doctor Alexander and Lou Jackson were made to pay fines of $25.00 a piece for their part in the festivities.

35

To Gain Spiritual Strength

FOR GAINING MORE AND BETTER SPIRITUAL PERCEPTION

This charm, according to Doctor Freddie Moses, is a great aid for sharpening the mind and for gaining a keener understanding of the spiritual world around you.Get a ***red flannel bag*** or ***a small chamois sack*** and fill it, with the following ingredients:

Lodestone	**1 piece**
Nutmeg Powder	**1/2 teaspoon**
Frankincense Incense	**1/2 teaspoon**
Orris Root Powder	**1/2 teaspoon**
Saltpeter	**A pinch**
Sandalwood Incense	**1 Teaspoon**
Uva Ursi	**A pinch**
Wood Bettany	**2 teaspoons**

Tie the top of the bag (don't sew it shut) and carry it in a pocket or a purse. Pour a little out and burn it each time you are ready to pray. This is said to guarantee a higher degree of spiritual strength. You may also wish to light a ***Spiritual White Candle*** while at home and preparing for bed at night.

Doctor Moses, mentioned previously, was a major Voodoo King in New Orleans of the 1940's. He ran an extremely profitable Voodoo mail-order business.

TO INCREASE YOUR SPIRITUAL POWER

This unusual talisman is the best one known to wear while contemplating and praying for spiritual assistance. It gives the possessor special powers to contact the spirit world for all sorts of advice in all matters of importance. It gives anyone who wears the talisman the ability to see through the intentions of others. Lastly, it aids judgement when dealing with anything in the spirituat realm. Embroider in ***orange silk on black satin*** and carry with you. It may also be engraved on a ring or an amulet.

Note: The sword stuck in the ground in the above talisman represents the Voodoo loa *Ogu*, who is said to have the greatest of weaknesses for pretty females. He always willingly gives his assistance to such girls before he will consider helping anyone else. The other symbols are simply made to help. direct the forces of *Ogu*. A special offering of a mango and some peanut oil are required when asking for this loa's assistance. Ogu is the favorite spirit force of all people asking for divine aid. He will refuse to take any action on your behalf should you forget to give him the proper offering.

TO GAIN MORE PSYCHIC ABILITY

Rose Powder	1/4 cup
Frankincense	1/2 cup
Sandalwood Incense	1/2 cup
Lavender Incense	3/4 cup
Orris Root Powder	1/2 cup
Cinnamon	2 teaspoons
Rosemary Leaves (powdered)	2 teaspoons
Queen Elizabeth Root	1 root

OR

Pimento Powder	1 teaspoon
Saltpeter	2 teaspoons
Patchouly Powder	1 cup
Sage Powder	1/4 cup
Allspice	1/2 cup
Cinnamon	1 cup
Wood Bettany (crushed)	1 cup
Myrrh Incense	2 teaspoons
Orris Powder	1/2 cup
Orchid Powder	1/2 cup
Wormwood Powder	1/2 cup
Saffron Incense	2 teaspoons
Sandalwood Incense	1/3 cup

Blend either of the above groups of ingredients in a large bowl, cover tightly, and set aside in a cool dark place until needed. Burn 1 teaspoon of this mixture on a piece of ***Fast Lighting Charcoal*** every night as you prepare for bed. Keep a small piece of ***Queen's Root*** under your mattress, and a second piece in your pillow case.

Each morning upon arising, light some more of the incense while you draw your bath water. Add 9 drops of ***Attraction Oil*** to the water and then bathe. Dry off well and anoint our body with some ***Ju Ju Oil*** and then rub your forehead with a little ***Obeah Oil.*** Follow these directions carefully and, according to High Priestess Julia Jackson, the proper atmosphere of vibratory influences for a higher degree of psychic ability will surround you at all times. Jackson, mentioned previously, was without doubt the most powerful and financially successful Voodoo woman during the 1940's. She was shrewd, vicious and revengeful when crossed.

This woman practiced Voodoo in New Orleans for over 30 years and was respectfully called "Miss Julia," by all who came into contact with her. Although she claimed never to have hexed anyone to death, Jackson was feared by one and all, and she was even nicknamed "Black Lightning." Julia concocted all of her own Voodoo ingredients and would not buy any from the stores supplying this type of merchandise. She ended up owning half the property in the block on which she lived as a result of her massive Voodoo trade.

36

To Get and Hold a Job

TO HELP FIND A GOOD JOB

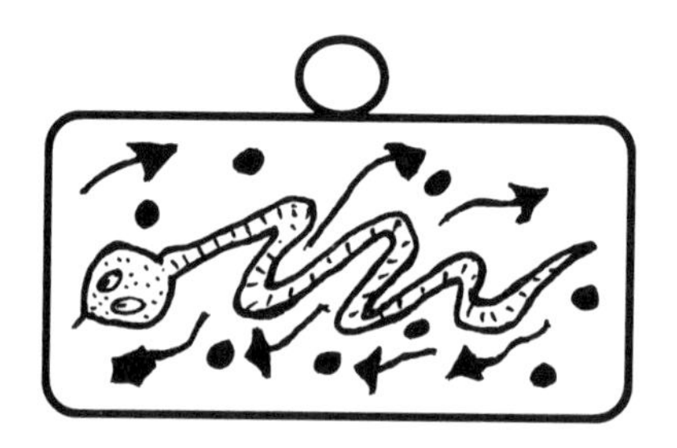

This potent talisman brings the possessor good luck when he or she is searching for suitable employment. And it opens many important doors when the need arises. It brings helpful spirit forces to the aid of all people who wish to find a new job. Embroider in ***light green silk on silver satin*** and carry with you. It may also be engraved on a ring or an amulet.

Note: The large headed snake with spots in the above talisman represents the Voodoo loa Petro *simi,* who can accomplish anything a believer wants done concerning a job. The other symbols are simply made to intensify *Petro* Simi's powerful forces and to help direct them when needed. This spirit requires an offering of white wine and homemade bread before he can be induced to take action in your behalf. Never try to use this talisman for any other purposes than directed above or the wrath of Petro *Simi* may turn upon you.

ED MURPHY'S RED CLOVER CHARM

*Take some dried and powdered **Red Clover** and place it in a **red flannel sack.** Add a **Lodestone** and sew the top of the bag tightly together. Carry this in your pocket or in a purse, or wear it on a string around your neck. Just before going on a job interview, or asking for a raise, sprinkle a little more Red Clover in your right shoe.*

This is another of Doctor Ed Murphy's special plant charms. Mentioned previously, Murphy attracted a wide and avid following for his conjure work in Mississippi of the 1920 period. He was born with a caul over his face and had 3 birthmarks on his left arm. These, he said, represented "Father, Son and Holy Ghost." A "good luck" mole could be seen on his right arm. Murphy meditated much of the time and claimed to have seen many visions which enabled him to accurately foresee the future.

DEVIL'S SHOE STRING CHARM

*Carry a piece of **Devil's Shoe String** in your pocket when seeking employment or even having problems on your job. Or, it may be worn on a plain **white cotton string** around your neck as a good luck amulet. Either way is said to bring luck while hunting a job, having an interview, or asking for a raise.*

This simple charm was popularly sold in the early 1850's by such High Priestessess as Madame Joyeau, Elizabeth Sutherland, and Madame Titite. They all worked their mystical art in New Orleans and each was in the employ of Marie Laveau for a period of time. These 3 Queens were big in their day and each one of them had a huge and loyal following.

MAMA LALA'S JOB'S TEARS CHARM

This is a simple yet effective job seeker's charm which is said to bring luck when being interviewed, or looking for work. And it is also of value when going to your boss for a raise in pay. Take some ***Job's Tears*** and hide them under your mattress. Place 7 more inside your pillow case. Leave them there for 7 days and then replace with fresh ones. Double the usual quantity when trying to get a big promotion.

The ***Job's Tears*** charm is credited to Mama Lala, although it was used by many others long before her time. Mama practiced Voodoo in New Orleans during the 1940's. She was a tiny dried up old black woman with prominent eyes, high cheekbones and fierce jagged looking yellowed teeth. She was usually seen wearing scuffed up men's shoes and long gray underwear which hung down below the hem of her dirty brown dress. A plain old shawl was held around her head by a decrepit safety pin under her chin. But no one dared laugh even though Lala may have appeared amusing. She was respected and feared by all for her evil power. This old crone lived in a small two room shanty full of religious pictures and a small altar well stocked with colorful candles.

DOCTOR DUKE'S FLOWER CHARM

Take some ***Camomile Flowers*** and place them in a ***small red flannel bag.*** Sew the top together tightly and attach a ***white cotton string.*** Wear around the neck whenever you are going out to look for a job or when asking for a raise. Also boil some of these same flowers in ***fresh rain water.*** Allow it to cool and then use this liquid as a good luck hand wash before entering into any kind of new employment venture. Do both of these things and you are said to always be successful.

This is another creation credited to the famous Doctor Duke who was mentioned previously. He went into the swamps and always gathered his own herbs and roots for use in making his charms. He was said to be good in giving legal assistance and often received hundreds of dollars for his Voodoo conjure work in this regard. Doctor Duke often used ***Goofer Dust or Graveyard Dirt*** as a part of his charms. He was very popular in his day and attracted a huge following.

37

To Conquer Troublesome People

CALLING ON DEMONS FOR ASSISTANCE

Marie Comtesse, mentioned previously, believed that demons could be called forth from the depths of darkness whenever she wished to cause harm to an enemy or a rival Queen. She began by carefully blending the following ingredients:

Black Arts Incense	**1 teaspoon**
Myrrh Powder	**1 teaspoon**
Doggrass	**1 teaspoon**
Dragon Blood Powder	**1 teaspoon**

These items are to be mixed only at midnight under the light of a full moon. When prepared, place half in an incense burner and light. Pour the other half in a ***red flannel bag*** and sew the top tightly together. Attach a ***white cotton string*** to the bag and hang it around your neck. Wearing this charm bag offers you protection while the invoked demons are close at hand. As the incense smolders, repeat aloud the following invocation:

O powerful demons of the deep
Come harm mine enemy as I sleep!
I command thee! I command thee!
Do your work well!
Go forth and destroy!

This particular cursing charm must be practiced with extreme caution. The person who invokes these demons must retain his or her composure throughout the entire ceremony. Complete control must be retained as the demons appear or they may turn instead on the person giving the invocation. No sign of fear or weakness must be given at this point.

Queen Marie Comtesse, as noted before, ended most of her popular Voodoo rituals with uninhibited sex games. These were participated in both by those involved in the ceremony and those who attended simply to observe. The New Orleans Times Democrat reported on one such out of door festivity when they wrote: "The rites consisted in building a large fire, in a dance . . . the destruction of a black cat and its devouring raw, the scene concluded with an orgy, in which the savage actors ended by tearing off their garments."

TO STOP ENEMIES

This talisman is said to disarm an enemy and make him powerless to inflict harm on the possessor. It forces others to their knees in subjugation to your every will and whim. Embroider in ***fire red silk on gold satin*** and carry with you. It may also be engraved on a ring or amulet.

Note: The goat represents the Voodoo loa *Guede*, a spirit of death, sorcery and black magic. He has unlimited power to use for overcoming all people who cause the wearer trouble. *Guede* is strong and quite destructive when his forces are unleashed. His strength must in all cases be used with caution and then only whenabsolutely necessary. The two large eyes denote the all encompassing power of Guede. He cannot be thwarted by any other spirit. The other symbols are simply made to contain and direct his power. Guede requires an offering of goat's milk and black rooster blood before he will take any action on a believer's behalf.

TO QUICKLY GET RID OF A DREADED ENEMY

This is an old hexing method attributed to the notorious Papa Felix. Take a small piece of ***pure parchment paper*** and write down your enemy's name, 9 times, with ***Dove's Blood Ink.*** Light ***1 Double Action Reverse Candle (black)*** and allow this to burn for 1 full hour, no more or no less. While the candle flickers, blend the following ingredients:

Snake Root Powder	**1 teaspoon**
Clippings of Enemy's Hair	**9 pieces**
Fingernail Parings (enemy's)	**9 pieces**
Graveyard Dust	**2 teaspoons**
Poke Root Powder	**1 teaspoon**

After the candle has burned for the complete hour, blow it out. Then place it in a saucepan and melt the wax down. Mix the above blend in the hot wax and then put in the parchment paper. Allow to cool slightly and then thoroughly knead the black wax with all the other items and form it into the shape of a ball. Set aside in a cool dark place to harden. When it is hard, walk down to a river or a creek and toss the ball in over your left shoulder. Repeat the name of your cursed enemy as the ball is thrown. Walk slowly away and never glance back. This potent charm is said to either kill an enemy or at least make him so miserable that he will move far away from you.

Papa Felix was an unbelievably cruel Voodoo King who practiced his dastardly brand of this art during the late 1800's and early 1900's. He held most of his rituals in his own house and he was feared by all who came into contact with him. Felix always required a live black cat for all major ceremonies. The cat was boiled alive while surrounded with colorful candles. Then upon its death, Felix quickly removed the cat from the kettle and bit clean through its throat. He then proceeded to skin the cat with his teeth. After this the meat was equally divided among those in attendance and eaten. Lastly, the bones were saved for use as protective charms.

38

To Gain Peace of Mind

TO DESTROY MENTAL ILLNESS

This talisman is popular in Voodoo because it is said to have the power of clearing up all forms of mental illness. Rebellious spirits are believed to cause insanity. Such spirits will be compelled to stop their dangerous machinations. Embroider in ***silver silk on rose colored satin*** and place on the insane person. It may also be engraved on a ring or an amulet.

Note: The coiled snake represents the Voodoo loa *Guede Double*, the all powerful serpent god. He can overcome all mental anguish and he endows the wearer of this talisman with clairvoyant powers. The four barbed hooks surrounding *Guede Double* direct his forces, and the crosses make him work only for good. This loa requires an offering of black-eyed peas and boiled rice before he will take any action on your behalf. Never use this talisman for any other purpose than is directed above.

TO GAIN MENTAL HARMONY

White Clover (powdered)	**1 teaspoon**
Blue Vervain	**1 teaspoon**
Broom Herb	**1 teaspoon**
Uncrossing Oil	**10 drops**
Peace Oil	**10 drops**
Dragon Blood Bath Crystals	**1 packet**
Uncrossing Incense	**1 packet**

Father Watson gave these instructions to his followers: Blend the first 3 ingredients in a small jar, shake well, then add to 1 quart of lukewarm water. Hide this in a dark closet corner and leave it for 3 full days. Take it out of the closet on the fourth day and strain through a piece of muslin. Then stir in the ***Uncrossing Oil and the Peace Oil,*** shake thoroughly and set aside until needed. Always shake the mixture before it is used.

You must take a daily bath in warm water to which has been added 1 teaspoon of the above mixture and 1 teaspoon of ***Dragon Blood Bath Crystals.*** As you are bathing, burn a small amount of the *Uncrossing Incense* close to the tub.

Do this complete ritual each day for 10 consecutive days; your mind is said to clear at the end of this time, if not before. Reverend Father Joe Watson, mentioned previously, gained a colorful reputation as a healer and powerful Voodoo man in New Orleans of the 1930's. He always wore a royal purple satin robe with a gold sash when holding services or rituals. Watson claimed to be able to curse or hex anyone at anytime and he believed that no one was powerful enough to break his hexes. He also bragged that he was able to lift any curse no matter which Voodoo King or Queen placed it. Father Joe had tremendous sex appeal and was both magnetic and hypnotic with the ladies. He made much money with his "high class" or "uptown" brand of Voodoo, and he sold special packets of powder as well as various charms for as little as $5.00 each.

HOW DOCTOR JOHN OVERCAME WORRY

CumminSeed	**1 teaspoon**
Peace Water	**1 pint**
Orris Powder	**1 packet**
Seven Day Peace Candle	**1**
Peace Incense	**1 packet**
Oil of Bergamot	**1 bottle**
Peace Powder	**1 packet**
Jinx Removing Powder	**1 packet**

Doctor John seems to have had answers for every kind of problem. First put the ***Cummin Seed*** in the jar of ***Peace Water,*** shake it well, and then leave it to soak for 3 full days in a dark cool place. Strain through a piece of muslin on the fourth day. Sprinkle 7 drops of this mixture in every corner of each room in the house. Anoint your forehead with some of this same mixture.

Now blend the **Orris Powder** and **Peace Powder.** Burn 1 teaspoon of this each evening when the sun goes down and light the **Seven Day Peace Candle.** The candle must be left alone to burn itself out.

Upon arising in the morning, rub some ***Oil of Bergamot*** on your forehead and in back of your ears. Sprinkle some ***Peace Powder*** on your hands and rub it over your naked body, especially over the chest and shoulder area. Then walk around the house or apartment and lightly sprinkle ***Jinx Removing Powder*** in each room. Do the same around the exterior of the house after you have dressed for the day.

Doctor John, mentioned previously, maintained a house full of embalmed snakes, scorpions and other horrifying items he needed to practice his special Voodoo magic. He also kept a statue of the Virgin Mary in his home, as well as dried toads nailed all over the walls. Doctor John was without doubt one of the most colorful Voodoo Priests in his day. He died at the age of 82 and Harpers Weekly said: "In the death of John Montanet, at the age of nearly a hundred years, New Orleans lost, at the end of August, the most extraordinary African character that ever obtained celebrity within her limits."

39

To Keep a Place Rented

TO ATTRACT RELIABLE LONG-TERM RENTERS

Bayberry Powder	**2 teaspoons**
Orris Powder	**2 teaspoons**
Spearmint (powdered)	**2 teaspoons**
House Blessing Powder	**1/4 Cup**
Sandalwood Incense	**1/4 Cup**
Attraction Incense	**1/2 cup**
Red Clover (crushed)	**1 teaspoon**

Blend all of the above ingredients in a wooden bowl, cover tightly, and set aside in a bright cheery corner until needed. Then scrub all the floors of the place to be rented. Use lukewarm water mixed with some ***Van Van Floor Wash.*** Then rub some ***Spring Mint Oil*** on each door knob of the house or apartment. Anoint your forehead with ***Success Oil*** and rub a little of this same oil on your palms. After carefully following all of these directions, put a little of the previously prepared incense mixture on a number of plain white saucers. You will need one for each room in the place to be rented. Place the saucers in the center of each of the rooms and light the incense.

This special charm is said to always attract good rental prospects. It was used back in the 1930's by Rockford Lewis, who was released in 1936 from the Federal Penitentary in Atlanta, Georgia, after having served his 2 year stretch for mail fraud. Lewis was at this time 31 years old and eager to regain his former stature in the Voodoo world. Rockford immediately returned to New Orleans and opened up his Voodoo "drug store" on Royal Street. Then in 1938, he again decided to go nationwide and reinstituted his mail-order racket.

TO RENT A PLACE REGULARLY

This excellent old-time talisman should be used by anyone who has a house, apartment or rooms to rent. It attracts reliable renters and even prospective purchases when a place is up for sale. Good spirit Forces will draw people to any place where the landlord needs assistance. Embroider in ***purple silk on yellow satin*** and carry with you. It may also be engraved on a ring or an amulet.

Note: The tree in the above talisman represents the *Voodoo loa Alivodu,* a good spirit who protects buildings and property to be rented or leased. The other symbols are simply made to intensify and direct his forces when the lea is called upon to take action. *Alivodu* requires an offering of dried herbs or leaves to make him happy, before he will act in the wearer's behalf.

Helping Yourself with
Magickal Oils
A-Z
Maria
Solomon

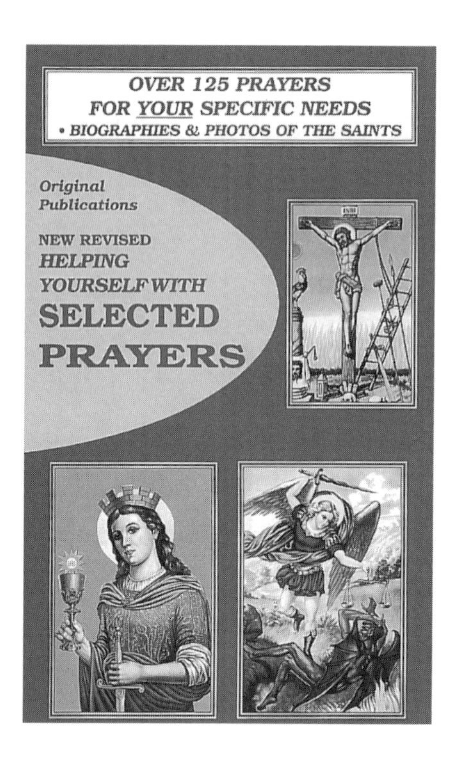

Now over **75,000** in print, ***The New Revised Helping Yourself with Selected Prayers*** provides an English translation for over 125 prayers of various religious beliefs. These prayers will provide a foundation upon which you can build your faith and beliefs. It is through this faith that your prayers will be fulfilled.

An index is provided to help the reader find the appropriate prayer for his or her particular request. The index also includes suggestions regarding the appropriate candle to burn while saying a particular prayer.

The devotions within these pages will help you pray consciously, vigorously, sincerely and honestly. True prayer can only come from within yourself.

112 pages, paperback, $4.95

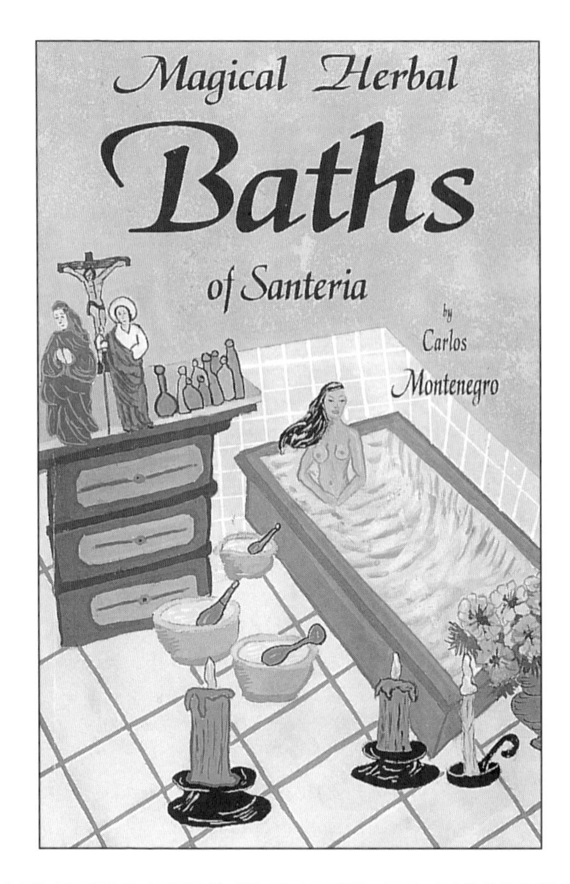

MAGICAL HERBAL BATHS OF SANTERIA

by Carlos Montenegro

One of the reasons that Santeria has become so popular is due to the use of natural remedies and herbal medicines prepared by the Santero Priests. By combining elements of spirituality with that of nature, a Santero Priest can accomplish great success with even the most difficult case. Spiritual herbal baths are widely used in the Santeria religion. Although all of the ingredients are natural, when combined with powerful supernatural magic, these herbal baths can produce incredible results. Spiritual baths have been used for hundreds of years to heal sickness and for supernatural power. The Montenegro Family has been practicing Santeria for over 200 years. This book explores the mysteries and techniques of preparing herbal baths used in traditional Santeria. The book contains lists of herbs, oils, powders, rituals and other magical ingredients used by Santeros for hundreds of years. *Orisha baths, love baths, money baths, cleansing baths, sweet baths and also baths used in Palo Mayombe and traditional Mexican witchcraft.* $5.95

voodoo